Change:

How to adapt and
transform the business

Change:

How to adapt and transform the business

Editor
N. Anand
London Business School

Series Editor
Nigel Nicholson
London Business School

Change:
How to adapt and transform the business

Published by
Format Publishing
31 Cattle Market Street
Norwich
NR1 3DY

ISBN 1903091381

First published 2004

British Library Cataloguing in Publication data
A CIP record for this book is available from the British Library

Series Editor
Nigel Nicholson

Editor
N. Anand

Additional editorial and writing
Tom Albrighton, Bernadette Sheehan

Cover design
Matthew Knight

Page design
Kaarin Wall

Set in Sabon and MetaPlus

Cover image
Sossusvlei, Namib Desert, Namibia, Africa
by Digital Vision/Getty Images

Page images
Getty Images

Printed
In the UK by Norwich Colour Print on paper derived from forests sustained with ‘two-for-one’ planting

Contents

How to use this book:

- Each chapter deals with a broad area of focus, set out in the panel on its first page.
- Within each chapter are a number of modules dealing with smaller areas of focus. In some cases, modules have 'Read more' links (see below).
- At the end of each chapter, a 'Looking back' panel summarises the key points.
- Chapters and modules are listed in the contents. The index lists all topics in alphabetical order.
- 'Real life' panels present examples and relate them to concepts in the text.

Read more:

- You can find out more about the ideas and examples in this book by following 'Read more' links.
- 'Read more' links take the form of a simple title and author reference at the end of the relevant section.
- To find out more about the work referenced, and (where applicable) buy it online, visit **www.formatpublishing.co.uk**

Introduction

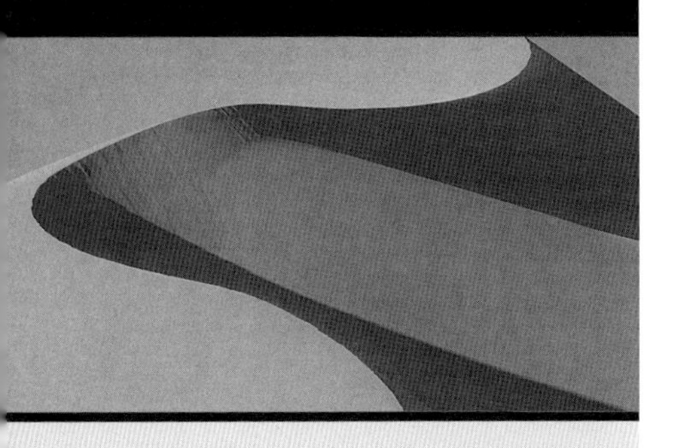

by Nigel Nicholson

The subject of this book is change, a topic it is easy today to conceive of as universal. We are forever being told not only to expect change to be a constant aspect of business life, but also to expect it to accelerate as innovation and technology gallop faster along an exponential growth trajectory. This is quite scary. Indeed, increasingly, one hears of 'burnout', 'change fatigue', 'overwork', 'crises of confidence' and 'cultures of cynicism'. These are real twenty-first-century phenomena. How will another book on change help?

A first consideration is that any truly helpful book on the topic will be as much about stability and preservation as it is about change and revolution. It is futile just to try to chase the whirligig of change at ever-faster speeds. Rather, we need to gain mastery over its motion and to understand the seasons of change, so that we can drive change when we want or need to, and so that we know when it is necessary and desirable to put the brakes on. In an ideal world we should seek change for what it brings us, not because we feel it is intrinsically necessary. We need to be able to embrace change without the fearful feeling that it brings all costs and no gain.

But the reality is that people have good reason to be fearful, cynical and disillusioned. On all sides business changes are disappointing people, because:

- what is **promised** is not delivered
- the **pain** outweighs the **gain**
- long-term interests are sacrificed to **short-term objectives**
- **cosmetic change** substitutes for dealing with fundamentals
- people make **sacrifices** and are then cast aside
- change is driven by **executive ego** not business need
- loyal, hard-working employees bear all the **costs**
- changes don't **last**
- **leaders disengage** when things go wrong
- change agents don't **walk the talk.**

One could add to this list but it would serve no purpose. The point here is that all of these are avoidable through good management, far-sightedness and a strategic orientation to change. This book sets out how to achieve this, drawing on the latest management thinking, academic theory and observed best practice.

Some themes are worth noting. First is that change has always been a constant in human life. We humans are highly change-adaptable animals, used to pulling together to face crises, accommodating elemental forces and following the rhythm of the seasons. We are also creative creatures, continually seeking improvements to our way of life, implementing innovations and seeking novelty. It is a myth that people hate change. It is not hard to encourage people to embrace change, but they have to believe that it promises an improvement in the status quo, and that no change is the undesirable option.

But people do resist change. The list above supplies ample reason. It boils down to a lack of trust and belief. People are wary of change that asks them to accept uncertainty and possible loss in exchange for abandoning comfort, adjustment and their familiar network of relationships and operations. It is not that most of us are entirely contented with the status quo. Most people's work situations are full of imperfections but their inner voice reasons 'better the devil you know…'

Trust is also undermined by poor or absent relationships with the people who are driving change, mistrust of their motives, and negative memories of past experiences with them. Put these together and it becomes clear that resistance to change is the rational response to change proposals, until and unless they can be proved to be trustworthy. The burden of proof is with the prosecution, not the defence.

Yet the pressures for change are indeed inexorable. Globalisation is the principal force shaping many businesses, with barriers to entry and to competition falling away sharply in almost all sectors. Even in the not-for-profit area, the knock-on effects of the sweeping social and technological changes that characterise our era are altering and often increasing the demands faced by staff and their leaders.

Under these circumstances the challenge is to gain mastery over change and to avoid being its victims, so that we shape the future rather than it bending us out of shape.

How can we do this? Where do change leaders go wrong? How can we do better?

A chief source of difficulty and failure is that executives approach change management as if it were a technical project. Their reasoning runs: if you know where you need to get to, you have only to plot the route and start the engine. This no-nonsense approach appeals to many of today's business leaders. These are mainly people (men mainly) with a single-minded, driven approach to leadership, a determination not to get left behind, and a simple faith that good ideas and strategies will be accepted by any reasonable person. The people who resist are, thus, by definition unreasonable and must either be dumped or converted.

The reality, as savvy change agents know, is that we have to deal with change as a matter of the heart as much as of the head. People's anxieties have to be surfaced and addressed, which may be difficult in organisational cultures characterised by rationality and emotional inhibition, as is the case in many firms. Change management is also about what is going on in people's heads – especially the prevalence of false beliefs. As the sociologist W.I. Thomas noted, 'what is taken to be real is real in its consequences'.

This means that change agents have not only to plot a realistic path, but they also have to mobilise hearts and minds through effective communication strategies. There are three elements to communication, each of which can fatally break down:

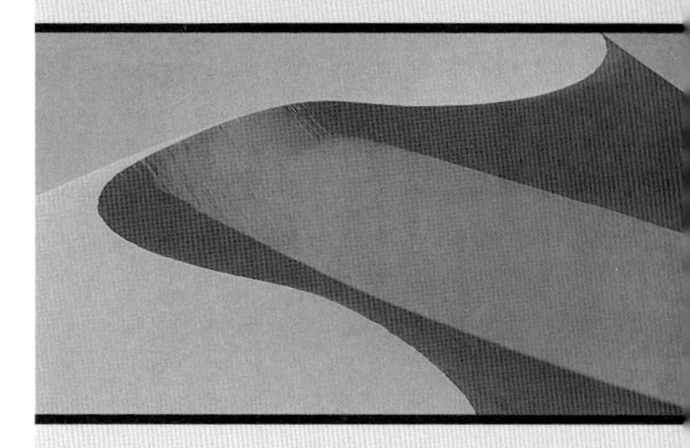

- **encoder quality:** how the message is framed
- **decoder receptivity:** the willingness and ability of people to receive the message
- **channel quality:** the appropriateness of the medium and its freedom from noise.

Change leaders tend to focus mostly on encoding – honing their messages – and secondly on channels – creating the most attractive delivery mechanisms. What they tend to ignore is receptivity – the interests, expectations and prior beliefs of their audience, and the fact that the most attended-to communications come from networks of gossip.

It is for this reason that much of this volume is concerned with issues of culture, since it is the norms, values, practices and language of relationships in organisations that makes change possible, successful and beneficial. ■

1 Overview

This chapter looks at what change is and when it happens, why managing it is essential, why change often fails, and what we can learn from one company that has prospered through successful change.

About change

Change is the process of altering, reshaping or transforming a business to improve the way it works or interacts with its environment.

Businesses that want to grow, diversify or simply survive in today's fast-moving business environments have to change more quickly than ever before. Change has become a constant; it's no longer a one-off or an exception to 'normal life'. The ability to manage change effectively, to bring real benefit to the business, is an essential skill for all decision makers.

The next chapter looks in detail at why change becomes necessary. Briefly, the main reasons are:

- **new environments:** competitors increase the pressure; markets change; society changes; customers and their needs change
- **new directions:** new products and services; new ways of working
- **new growth:** the business gets bigger, either by gradual evolution or through a deliberate effort, and has to change as a result

- **new cultures:** changes in structures and processes require parallel changes in the way people work together if the business is to reach its full potential.

Without careful management, change can become a business nightmare. New structures and processes are imposed without enough forethought, people don't understand what is being aimed for or what is expected of them, and those in charge get bogged down in endless details and compromises. Change becomes an unfocused, indefinite time of turmoil. Having started without direction and continued without focus or monitoring, it ends in a whimper when those involved can go no further.

This book will give you an overview of the elements of change management, including what is involved at each stage of change, and point the way towards the key techniques that you will need to make successful changes in your business. It is aimed at those involved in change as much as those managing it, since an understanding of the best way to manage change can be useful no matter what level of the business you work at.

Why changes fail

Many change initiatives fail. They start brightly, with affirmations of the need to change, new structure charts, vision statements and business plans, but gradually lose momentum. Old ways and structures slowly reassert themselves, managers seem to lose heart or become distracted by new problems, and the business drifts back to its former state. Why does this happen, when change is essential?

Change fails because managing it is one of the most demanding tasks in business. It requires the full range of management skills: 'hard' skills in planning, project management and analysis, and 'soft' skills in persuasion, understanding business cultures and communication. Many efforts at transformation fail because they neglect the human side of change.

The reasons for change failing are often complex and will vary from business to business, but there are certain common themes. These are the mistakes that are all too easy to make when planning and managing change. However, they point the way toward the key techniques for managing changes successfully.

Real life : Changing for the better at Nokia

Finnish mobile telephone giant Nokia has become a household name. As a business, it has plenty to teach us about change: adapting to market forces, taking opportunities, restructuring internally and a sequence of diversifications and consolidations. The company has responded to (and made) many changes, with some hard times along the way, to arrive at its present position of market leader in the mobile phone market.

The Nokia company came into being in 1967 through the merger of existing businesses trading in paper, rubber and cables for power and communication. During the 1970s, the cable business led Nokia into research into semiconductors and innovations in digital telephone exchanges. These led to the creation of the network infrastructure that would form the basis of Nokia's success.

Nokia was quick to pick up on changes in Finnish legislation allowing the creation of a car phone network. They created Nordic Mobile Telephony, the world's first multinational cellular network. In the late 80s, a common standard for digital mobile telephony was developed – GSM. Quick on the uptake again, Nokia moved

in and by 1991 supplied GSM networks to 59 operators in 31 countries.

During the 80s, Nokia diversified its business. It developed a diverse portfolio of businesses, including TV and IT, but the subsequent recession of the early 90s hit the company hard. It changed tack, divesting its non-core interests and choosing to concentrate solely on telecommunications. The strategy paid off: in the eight years from 1992 to 2000 it went from being in the doldrums to becoming a global leader in mobile telephony.

Key aspects of the Nokia story include:

- **radical change can secure success:** to ensure its future, Nokia has boldly transformed itself again and again, changing its structure from a single business to a conglomerate and back to a single business
- **adapt to the environment:** a big part of Nokia's success has been its willingness and ability to move between markets in response to social and economic change, and to view such changes as opportunities rather than threats
- **culture is crucial:** Nokia is renowned for preserving the 'feel' of a small company despite its size; it understands the business benefits of shared values and approaches and recognises the need to manage business culture actively.

Management guru John Kotter suggests eight reasons for change failure:

- **allowing too much complacency:** change gets its momentum from a sense of urgency and a keen awareness of problems
- **failing to create a sufficiently powerful guiding coalition:** strong leadership, with involvement from those at the top of the business, is essential
- **underestimating the power of vision:** a compelling vision is invaluable in guiding, aligning and inspiring actions for change
- **undercommunication:** motivation and commitment depend on understanding and belief in the benefits of change, which can only be achieved through communication
- **allowing obstacles to remain:** there will be obstacles (practical and cultural) to change; they have to be confronted rather than accepted if change is to succeed
- **not going for quick wins:** commitment and enthusiasm are boosted when people can see benefits arising from change early in the process

- **declaring victory too soon:** effort has to continue until change has taken root in the business's culture, and performance has been shown to improve; otherwise the business will go back to its old ways
- **failing to anchor change culturally:** change has to be rooted in shared values, not just shared hierarchies and processes; it needs to become 'the way we do things around here'.

Note that most of these are to do with people. It is not changes to plans, procedures and hierarchies that are most difficult to implement; it is the changes in people's minds. If the case for change has not been identified and communicated, it will be hard to generate focus, enthusiasm and motivation. If people cannot see the personal benefit in making a change work, they will resist it, or actively oppose it. If no one believes in the change, no one will get behind it.

All these factors originate within the business. Outside forces can also push a change off course. Reasons for failure originating outside the business include:

- failing to anticipate or respond to new **competition**
- failure to take account of factors in the **business environment:** changes to markets; changes in standard industry practice; shifts in the industry mindset
- failure to understand or predict the wider **social context:** for example, dependence on favourable regulation; reliance on growth linked to shifting social and/or economic trends
- over-dependence on key **resources:** making a change that depends on potentially unreliable or insufficient resources in areas such as consultancy skills, manpower, raw materials or energy

- poor **founding conditions**: for example, partnerships or joint ventures that are set up without adequate resources or backing from the founding organisations
- bad **network location**: having key facilities in places where vital resources are not available – transport links and key suppliers, for example.

If change does fail – for whatever reason – the cultural consequences can be profound. Failure may generate the perception that the business is incapable of changing, that change is not worthwhile or is somehow optional, that management aren't really in control, or that a negative situation cannot be turned round. The kind of attitudes that will be reinforced as a result are likely to make changes even more difficult in the future.

Read more:

Leading Change

by John P. Kotter

Looking back:

Key ideas from this chapter

- Reshaping the business to adapt to a changing environment is an essential part of management.
- Change has to be actively managed if it is to be successful and bring benefits.
- Change often fails; the reasons for failure illustrate the keys to success.
- The most successful companies manage change well and look for opportunities for changing rather than waiting for change to be forced upon them.

2 Origins

You need to understand where change comes from in order to build a foundation for generating commitment, defining success, planning effectively and overcoming resistance.

The reasons for change

It is important to be clear on the reasons why change is necessary. Even in situations where it seems obvious what needs to be done, returning to the source of change is always worthwhile. Identifying, emphasising and reiterating the key issues that change needs to address has several positive effects:

- it helps to **generate enthusiasm** for change (at least among those who understand and accept the reasons put forward)
- it helps to **align and focus** change efforts, particularly where resource is limited, on the things that really will make a difference
- later on, it makes it easier to **gauge success** – that is, whether change really did address the issues you identified at the outset.

Focusing effort is an important part of effective change management. It is all too easy – perhaps even tempting – to be sidetracked by side benefits or opportunistic changes. These may lead you into actions that cure symptoms rather than causes, with the result that your change effort produces a 'quick fix' that fails to address what is really troubling the business.

The reasons for change will be unique to your business. Every organisation has different issues and situations to which it needs to respond. Developments that may prompt changes include:

- **competitor activity**: imitation of products or services by others; competition on price; being outflanked in the market
- changes in **customer profile**:
  - **increased choice**: customers increasingly expect to find a choice of suppliers and/or products rather than a single option
  - **higher expectations**: good quality and good service have become much more widely expected
  - **increased affluence**: for example, as people have become more well-off, a lesser share of disposable income has gone to clothing and more towards newer retailers of consumer electronics and luxury goods
- changes in **market profile**: growth or decline of a market; different environment; different prevailing attitudes; different sectors
- **expectations** of directors, chief executive and/or shareholders not being met (or not being met quickly enough)
- **growth and expansion**: larger number of customers; new kinds of customers; new ventures; new products and services; spin-offs from existing business lines; mergers and acquisitions; failed attempts at international expansion
- **poor performance**: falling turnover; slimmer margins; losing customers
- **need for revitalisation**: executing a turnaround of a declining business; creating customer focus in a successful business
- **need for cultural renewal**: low morale; increasing staff turnover; lack of identification with the business among staff; innovative ideas not being generated; culture at odds with what is required for the business environment, or with what customers expect
- **need for new alliances**: establishing partnerships with other businesses; taking advantage of global markets; 'co-opetition' (working together with companies who are nominally competitors for mutual benefit).

No reason for changing is inherently 'better' than any other – all businesses are different – but people within the business may assign much more importance or credibility to certain reasons than they do to others. For example, it may be much harder to make a case for (and achieve) a cultural change, even though this kind of 'soft' change is no less likely to increase competitive advantage than an aggressive programme of cost-cutting and performance management. Those with a financial management perspective, for example, are likely to instinctively favour the latter, which they may feel is most closely linked with the area they understand and wish to see changing. The next chapter looks in more detail at how the reasons for change need to be presented in order to generate commitment to the change effort.

Proactive and reactive change

Some change efforts are proactive. These are situations where the business takes the lead in deciding its own future: moving into new business areas, forging new alliances or cultural transformation. Proactive change is characterised by seeking out reasons for change, rather than waiting for them to arise. Other changes are reactive; they are taken in response to events such as market changes, new competition and changing customer priorities as and when they occur.

There is one major benefit to changing proactively: you have more time. Planning in advance gives you much more flexibility over options, priorities, resources and timescales. The earlier problems are foreseen and dealt with, the easier it will be to make the necessary changes.

Crises

At the extreme of reactive change is the need to respond to a crisis situation, where a single critical event or situation obliges a business to change. In a well-managed business, crises are likely to originate from uncontrollable or unforeseen factors outside the business: most internal crises should be known about before they occur.

Crises usually make some kind of change unavoidable, even if it's only a temporary transformation. This has the potential to be positive for the business, but the 'crisis mentality' can make good change management very difficult.
Crisis problems include:

- the desire to find a solution quickly moves the emphasis from long-term, strategic thought to **short-term, tactical solutions** that may not safeguard the future of the business (or could even harm it)
- the need for swift, focused, unambiguous action makes it more likely that change will be **non-participative** – perhaps led by a single individual who may or may not understand the wider consequences of their actions; the long-term cultural effects of people not being involved in the change may be significant
- the heat of the moment can make bold measures, ill-considered **risks** and 'big bang' transformational changes seem more appropriate than they really are.

Some businesses are characterised by a conservative, reactive and risk-averse approach that tends to favour caution over bold, proactive moves. But this approach in itself is risky, because it fails to address big issues until they become crises. The business is then forced into taking risks in haste and without enough thought.

Any of the crisis responses listed above may lead to changes being made that are unsustainable, with the business reverting to old ways once the crisis is passed. That's why it is so important, difficult though it may be, to use crises as opportunities to find out what positive transformations can be made:

- acknowledge the full extent and nature of the **problem**; look for the true causes of the crisis; resist the temptation to view persistent problems as isolated incidents
- acknowledge **mistakes** made; identify the strategies and decisions that have led to the crisis (but draw a line under the past and refrain from blame)
- look at how **information** moves within the business – someone usually knows about crises before they happen; consider how information could be used more effectively in the future; encourage and reward communication and knowledge sharing between departments and teams.

Real life : Time for a change at M&S

Marks and Spencer grew from humble beginnings in 1884 to become a household name in clothing and (more recently) food retail. A very successful brand, a reputation for quality and low costs through careful supplier management have all helped to preserve the company's strong position.

Marks and Spencer successfully navigated the recession of the early 90s, delivering year-on-year growth and retaining stability. By 1994 its turnover was £6.5 billion. But things started to go wrong in the late 90s, with profits declining and business in the UK suffering. The need for change was clear.

The drivers for change included:

- **changing customer expectations**: customers increasingly expected more and more choice; they were less likely to rely on a single established brand
- **changing perceptions**: the M&S brand (traditional, reliable, quality), once a key asset, began to seem more of a liability as markets changed
- **competitor activity**: other companies successfully imitated M&S's ideas
- **the rate of change**: fashions were beginning to change more quickly; M&S's development cycle struggled to keep up

The drivers for stability centred around the culture of the business:

- **conservatism and risk aversion**: a control-focused corporate style stifled innovation and discouraged criticism of management, so new directions could not arise
- **complacency and introspection**: the company's long history of success made people less likely to sense an urgent need for change
- **rigidity**: there were too many 'untouchables' within the business; tactics such as accepting only the company's own credit and debit cards were retained even though they increasingly irritated customers.

These signs were not heeded for some time, but around 2000 the company began to make changes to improve its position. The measures taken included:

- a new management team
- cost reduction
- increases in marketing and promotion
- some job cuts and closures
- general move towards a more outward-looking, change-focused culture.

Marks and Spencer still has its problems, and it remains to be seen whether it can effect the changes it needs to make through rebranding and other initiatives.

Whatever the outcome, there is an important lesson to be learned from the M&S story: seek out the reasons for change and act on them as soon as you can. Also, look to your own culture if change is failing or the business is faltering. An internal culture that starts out as a key strength can, if it is not changed when the time is right, end up being a supremely powerful constraint on the business and a major factor in its decline.

The force field

Force field analysis was created by social scientist and management thinker Kurt Lewin. This venerable technique is still used half a century after its creation, because it's a good way to get a handle on the reasons why your business needs to change, and the counterbalancing reasons why it remains as it is.

Force field analysis looks at the 'forces', or drivers, that act on a business. In the diagram overleaf, the business is the entity in the centre. Various drivers act on the business, with stronger or more significant drivers depicted as bigger. The direction of desired change is from left to right; drivers for change push the business in this direction, while drivers for stability (or those that resist change) push the business the opposite way.

The drivers shown might be relevant to a private or partnership firm that needs to adapt its services quickly, in a way that its culture cannot support. It might be a long-established firm of solicitors or a traditional retail operation. Competitors are at the door, and customers increasingly expect more, but the culture of the business is inward- and backward-looking. The lack of funds available right now, and the temptation to wait until the current MD retires, both make doing nothing an attractive option.

If the business is in a stable equilibrium (in other words, nothing much is changing right now), the forces are cancelling each other out. Making change happen is a matter of increasing the strength or number of the drivers for change, decreasing the drivers for stability, or a combination of both.

If your force field analysis doesn't look balanced, but your business isn't changing, you need to look again at the significance you've assigned to each force, or look for others that you may have missed. As always, the 'soft' factors shouldn't be neglected. If it looks like there is nothing 'concrete' to prevent change, or the case for

Force field analysis:

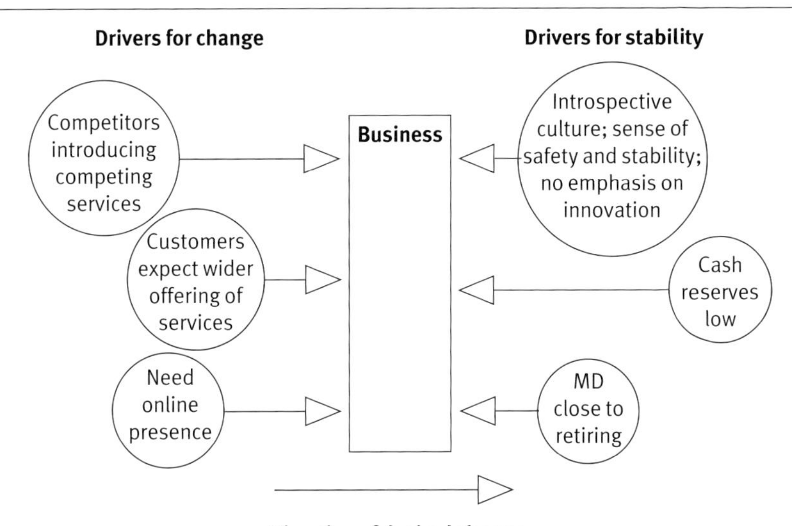

change looks overwhelming, consider what 'invisible' or cultural factors are helping keep the business where it is.

To help the business change, you need to strengthen or emphasise the drivers for change, while weakening or removing the drivers for stability. The result will be an increased impetus in the direction of change. So the analysis helps you understand what is pushing you on and holding you back, and suggests what kind of actions are needed to change that situation.

Many drivers for change come from outside the business, while drivers for stability often come from within it. Generating awareness of the need to change often involves shifting the focus to outside the business, or 'seeing yourself as others see you'. This includes increasing awareness of the business's culture, which can be a major driver for stability; the ways in which people think about the business can be a profound force holding it back (as in the example).

The force field technique can also be used to look at a particular option for the future or a proposed change. In this version, the option is at the centre of the diagram and the 'pros' and 'cons' are entered as 'forces'. Again, the different ways in which the option can be improved can be looked at in terms of lessening the 'cons' and/or improving the 'pros'.

Read more:

The Complete Social Scientist: A Kurt Lewin reader

edited by Martin Gold

Growing pains

It's usually taken for granted that every business wants to grow. Being bigger brings more security and stability, better responsiveness to customer needs, the potential to diversify, and many other positive changes. But growth can lead to problems if the organisation is not set up to cope with it: ways of doing things that were perfect at the time it was created can become inadequate or inappropriate later on. The things that made a smaller business successful – agility, responsiveness, adaptability and positive culture – can easily be compromised as the business grows.

Management consultant and writer Eric Flamholtz has identified ten very common symptoms of 'growing pains':

- ☐ people feel there are **not enough hours** in the day
- ☐ people spend too much time **'putting out fires'**
- ☐ people are **unaware of what others do**
- ☐ people don't understand the business's **goals**
- ☐ there are not enough good **managers**
- ☐ people think 'if I want something doing, I have to **do it myself**'

Growing pains:

Stage	Problems arising	Abilities needed
New venture	☐ Need entrepreneurial 'spark' to create a business	☐ Define market need ☐ Satisfy market need with a product or service ☐ Build an organisation that can deliver the product or service
Expansion	☐ Demand outstrips ability to respond ☐ Infrastructure can't cope with growing demands on it	☐ Acquire resources ☐ Develop complex operational systems
Professionalisation	☐ Informal, ad hoc management no longer adequate ☐ Entrepreneurial business culture less appropriate for larger concern	☐ Plan and develop a strategy ☐ Develop organisational structure, processes and systems ☐ Define roles, responsibilities and performance goals ☐ Provide training and management development
Consolidation	☐ Culture becomes critical to success ☐ Growth makes it harder for everyone to share one vision ☐ Individuals interpret business culture to meet their own needs	☐ Diagnose what the culture is ☐ Develop explicit, formal ways of actively managing culture ☐ Focus on redefining and communicating culture

- ☐ people feel **meetings are pointless**
- ☐ there are **no plans**, or if there are plans they aren't followed up, so things often don't get done
- ☐ some people feel **insecure** about their place in the business
- ☐ sales have grown, but **profits** have not grown hand-in-hand with them.

If you can see one or more of these symptoms in your business, it may be experiencing the problems of growth.

Dealing with growth

What you need to do to respond to growth depends on which stage of development your business is at. Although every business is different, growth tends to follow recognisable stages, as shown in the table opposite (adapted from Eric Flamholtz and Yvonne Randle's book *Changing the Game*).

The stages up to consolidation represent the journey to becoming a professionally managed company. The stages beyond this (diversification, integration, decline and revitalisation) represent a different order of growth, and typically involve businesses that have grown very large. Many businesses will never reach this point, either because they stop growing or because they fail.

Wherever you are along the growth curve, the emphasis is on acquiring or developing the abilities to respond to new challenges. Because growth changes the nature of the business, these abilities are radically different from the ones that took the business through the previous stage. They need to be actively sought out, either through the founder of the business consciously changing their outlook, or through delegation and recruitment. This is likely to be a major change, both in terms of how the business is run and also its culture. Without this kind of change, the business will end up stuck between two stages, 'wanting' to grow but lacking the skills and perspectives to move forward.

Read more:

Changing the Game

by Eric G. Flamholtz and Yvonne Randle

Business evolution

Darwin said that it is not the species with the greatest strength, nor the one with the highest intelligence that survives, but the one that is most adaptable to change. This is just as true of businesses as it is of living things. It can be enlightening to look at the parallels, and consider the business as a 'living' inhabitant of a bigger, ever-changing picture rather than an isolated, unchanging and inanimate object.

Through evolution, organisms acquire advantages that safeguard the survival of their species. In the same way, businesses need to find ways of transforming themselves in order to survive. Both have to achieve a good 'fit' with their environment, and both have to find strategies to deal with competitors or predators.

But, in contrast to living things, businesses often go for upheaval rather than gradual development – revolution rather than evolution. A more constructive approach may be to regard change as the natural state for a business, made necessary by the continuous shifts in the competitive forces acting on it. The business can then be seen as an ever-evolving entity that changes as and when it needs to, or before it needs to, rather than after change has become unavoidable. In other words, change could be an everyday phenomenon, not an unusual or exceptional event. It follows that the ability to manage change would be a central skill for any decision maker in the business.

One way to achieve this is by making it part of everyday management to look for 'break-out' changes that take the business in new directions. In this model, change is the 'natural' option. It would be incumbent on those opposed to change to justify staying the same, rather than others making the case for change.

In theory, achieving a perfect fit with the business environment could mean making some kind of change, however small, every single day. But it's important to remember that businesses are made of people, and most people like some degree of stability and certainty in their working life. It is easier to have an endpoint for change, or 'resting points' along the way to a radical change, at which you can return to 'normal life' and take stock of the results of your actions. On a practical level it's also easier, as we'll see in the next chapter, to manage bounded changes than unbounded or ill-defined changes.

A compromise is the idea of 'punctuated equilibrium'. This concept ties in with current ideas about evolution in the natural world; it is now thought that long periods of evolutionary stability are intermittently disturbed by new species arising. In the punctuated equilibrium management model, changes are made as soon as possible, but they have carefully set boundaries so they don't go on forever and end up demoralising people. Changes are separated by periods of stability that provide the opportunity for the business to re-adapt to its environment. The aim of this approach is to achieve balance between the business need for constant change, the practical need for change to have boundaries and the human need for stability and certainty.

Disturbing the equilibrium

For the business, as for the living organism, too much stability can be a bad thing. If the business fails to adapt, it will stagnate, losing touch with the demands of its environment and ultimately becoming 'extinct', just like living things that fail to adapt to changes in the world around them.

Unfortunately, fear of the unknown or the sense that change brings the risk of loss can make people averse to change, regarding it as inherently dangerous. This feeling may also stem from a preference for relying on approaches that have worked in the past, rather than new ways that are unproven. All these are understandable human attitudes, and many are beneficial at certain times, but there is a limit to how long a business should remain in equilibrium. If too much time goes by, problems may arise, including:

- the business becomes **insular and introspective**; competitive forces are played down or ignored; new customer demands are ignored or not taken seriously; the business is regarded as invulnerable
- **change becomes unthinkable**; the status quo comes to be regarded as the only possible way for the business to exist
- **complacent people** or 'time-servers' like what they see and bed down for the long haul to retirement
- **ambitious or creative people** don't like what they see and go elsewhere, unable to find a rewarding role for themselves within the business.

Real life : Positive changes at HSBC

As we've seen, it is often more beneficial to anticipate the need for change rather than waiting for it to arise. A key part of modern leadership is actively seeking out opportunities to transform the business and move it forward, rather than merely fixing problems so that it remains where it is.

International banking corporation HSBC has achieved leadership in Hong Kong's highly competitive banking industry by anticipating change and positioning itself to be ready for new developments before they happen.

A crucial step for HSBC was the realisation that the bank could not expand much further within Hong Kong. This, coupled with the high operating costs in that region, led to the decision to expand overseas. In time this saw HSBC become a global enterprise, growing through acquisitions of strong national banks such as Midland in the UK. However, despite its size, HSBC remains responsive and agile, with a strong focus on customer needs. HSBC's strategy is readjusted constantly in order to stay in tune with its customers' expectations.

One aspect of HSBC's claims to 'think global, act local' and of being 'the world's local bank' is the active management of business culture. HSBC is run within a supportive atmosphere, with teamwork and mutual support encouraged and politics discouraged. Diversity within the workforce is also actively sought.

The company aims to tailor its operations to every part of the world in which it operates, and to learn from people in these different environments wherever possible. There is strong evidence that this is an area where business needs to improve, in action and in perception: a 2003 MORI poll in the UK found that 72% of the public think that companies do not pay enough attention to the communities in which they operate.

Another aspect of the global-local approach is HSBC's commitment to a wide range of activities worldwide to give something back to the community. These underscore the need to keep close to the local community in order to serve it better. Recent examples include:

- staff getting involved in charitable activities (45,000 hours' charity work by Hong Kong employees in 2003)
- working with KITEZH, a Russian community caring for orphans, to raise funds and improve profile
- significant donations to the ABC Hospital in Mexico, allowing for the construction of a new community clinic in Mexico City.

These initiatives also help to foster a positive organisational culture that is based on real actions, not just statements of intent. As Nigel Pate (Senior Manager, HSBC in the Community) puts it, 'If you do good, you feel good, and if you feel good, you do good'.

Sustained efforts to foster understanding of new business environments and customer expectations among staff led to the perceived need for 'soft' changes, such as more relaxed styles of dress within the company. Such cultural aspects are seen as vital for facilitating change and the development of the business.

All these factors lead to a cycle of innovation being stifled and the status quo being reinforced – a vicious circle of stasis. In this kind of situation, the equilibrium needs to be actively disturbed, through conscious effort, so that new things can start happening.

One good method for disturbing the equilibrium is to give individuals or small teams independence within the business. Goals are set, but the means for achieving them are not. This allows the members of the team to:

- **react freely** to the business environment, and adapt to it quickly
- act **outside established norms**; find new ways of doing things
- **innovate**; find new things for the business to do
- gain valuable **learning** from their experience, which can then be shared with others in the business or 'rolled out' to the organisation as a whole.

Many larger businesses have found lasting, sustainable success with this type of approach. In some cases they go so far as to have no common 'norms' across the business at all, relying instead on the initiative of small teams within the business to manage themselves. While useful in enabling innovation, this approach may bring problems in terms of a fragmented culture, or even a conflict between team loyalty and company loyalty.

For the smaller enterprise, this idea is more likely to take the form of a continued focus on those at the 'sharp end' of the business – those who deal directly with customers, perhaps. This helps to remove any barriers or buffers that may evolve between decision makers and competitive realities, ensuring that introspection and complacency do not take hold, and that decisions are based on facts rather than comfortable assumptions.

Whatever technique is used, the overarching theme is the need for management decisions to avoid focusing solely on internal realities, which can often reinforce existing ideas, and look to the outside world, the catalyst for new directions.

Doing nothing

Doing nothing is always an option. Delaying change for a while and carrying on with 'business as usual' can seem appealing. If the business has cashflow problems, change can seem like an expensive luxury when what you need to be doing is saving money; after all, you might trade your way out of trouble. Change can also look risky – gambling valuable resources when the need to conserve them is paramount. Why take on change management on top of all the day-to-day problems you have to deal with?

So doing nothing can look like the low-risk option. But in fact it's often the opposite. Inaction has its consequences just as action does. You have to consider what is really happening: will doing nothing mean that things stay as they are, or are they more likely to steadily worsen? Market situations can decline, good people can leave the 'sinking ship', competitors might perceive that the business is drifting or stagnating and move in for the kill, customers may become disillusioned or disappointed and go elsewhere. You need to assess how likely it is that the approaches that have brought you to your current situation will be successful in taking you out of it.

Looking at the real costs and implications of doing nothing, without any optimistic bias, can be sobering. Preserving things as they are has its costs – not big, one-off or upfront investments that look bad on balance sheets, but overheads that discreetly eat away at profits year after year. Do people spend time working round impractical business systems? Are valuable, creative people fire-fighting when they could be generating ideas and revenue? These are the symptoms of the need for change.

Finally, don't underestimate the positive cultural impact of making changes in difficult situations. While you need to avoid the risks involved in taking hasty or over-ambitious changes, remember that proactive action reinforces the impression of control and understanding. This can restore faith in the organisation's collective ability and willingness to change, and motivate people for further change and improvement. Conversely, caution can easily look like weakness or indecision.

Looking back:

Key ideas from this chapter

- ☐ Change becomes necessary for many reasons; competition is a key factor.
- ☐ Changing proactively makes planning easier.
- ☐ Drivers for stability (or reasons not to change) have to be taken into account.
- ☐ Growth brings its own unique problems.
- ☐ Comfortable states of equilibrium sometimes have to be disturbed so the business can move forward.
- ☐ Doing nothing carries its own risks.

3 First steps

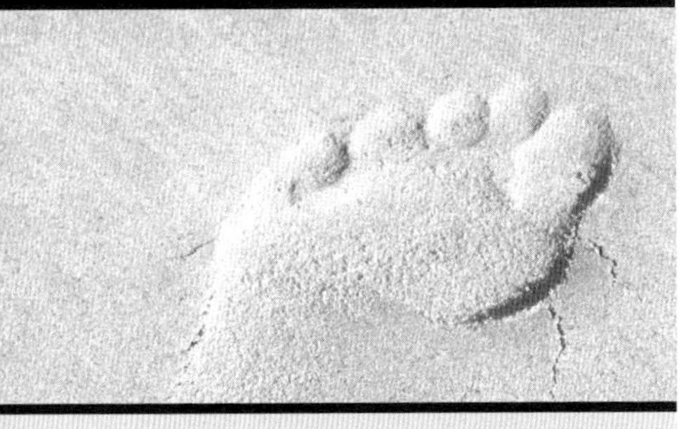

This chapter shows you how to prepare the ground for change: defining success, setting boundaries, identifying and analysing the key players in change and raising the heat.

Defining success

The first, crucial step in planning a change is to define its aim: the outcome that you want the change to bring about. Without clear aims, progress is likely to be slow and difficult, since agreement among those involved will be hard to achieve. Furthermore, there will be no way to tell when success has been achieved, which carries the risk that change continues indefinitely or drifts along without direction or closure.

Aims should identify what needs to change and why, and also define success: what will be different after the change; what constitutes a solution to the problem; the desired future state of the business or 'what it looks like when it works'.

Change aims should be simple. It should be easy to use them as guides when making decisions: to examine options by asking 'how will this help us achieve the changes we want?' The more complex and multi-dimensional your change aims are, the less effective they are likely to be in helping to create consensus, motivation and enthusiasm. A statement of aims doesn't have to include every detail of what's going to change – much of that may be undecided as yet – but it does need to unite and involve those who will be thinking about such details.

As the saying goes, 'to have more than one goal is to have no goal'. If possible, having a single aim for change is always going to be more effective than having two or more. If multiple aims are unavoidable, they must be consistent with one another, because any conflict between them will sooner or later lead to conflict between the people tasked with achieving them. Ideally, multiple aims should be brought together under a single unifying theme, inspiring for everyone involved but down-to-earth enough to make sense in terms of people's working realities.

Boundaries

The next vital step in planning change is to decide the boundaries of the change. Essentially this means deciding its scope: what is going to change and what isn't. It also means taking a broad view of the change and the factors that are likely to affect it.

Difficulties and messes:

Difficulties	Messes
□ Essentially bounded in scope	□ Essentially unbounded in scope
□ Limited number of people involved; easy to identify them	□ Not easy to identify all the people involved
□ Objectives of the change are clear and well understood	□ Objectives of the change are unclear; there is no agreement on objectives
□ Priorities for the change are clear	□ There is uncertainty or lack of agreement over priorities
□ Nature of the problem is clear, and so is what needs to change	□ Nature of the problem is not clear; there is disagreement over what the problem is and what needs to be changed
□ Relevant solutions are easily identified	□ Not clear what would constitute a 'solution'
□ All relevant information is known or accessible	□ Not clear what information is relevant, or information is unreliable or hard to find
□ Change effort is limited in timescale, or timescale is known	□ Longer timescale required, or timescale difficult to define

The potential problems of poorly defined boundaries are illustrated by Russell Ackoff's distinction between 'difficulties' and 'messes', shown in the table on the previous page.

Clearly, dealing with a difficulty is easier, more productive and less stressful than grappling with a mess. Whereas difficulties can be worked through logically and practically, with a clear solution in sight and all information to hand, messes are chaotic affairs characterised by confusion, lack of knowledge, poor communication and misunderstandings. Perhaps you recognise the characteristics of messes from badly managed changes that you have lived through. Many change efforts quickly become messes, or are messy from the outset. As a result they lose momentum or fail to address the problems they were intended to solve. This is problematic in itself, but also negatively affects attitudes and perceptions of people within the business.

To ensure that change (or any part of a change) does not become a mess, you must identify the following:

- the **aims** of change
- what **should be included**
- what **can be included** within present constraints (time, money, feasibility, etc)
- what **has to be excluded** (perhaps only for the time being, perhaps permanently)
- **who will be involved**: the best people for the tasks required; people whose work will be affected; people likely to have strong opinions (note that they may be outside the boundaries of the organisation)
- **who can be involved**: the constraints on the time, expertise and commitment that people will be able to offer
- the relevant figures of **authority** (not necessarily formal authority); how they relate to each other
- **milestones and timescales**: what you would like to have achieved at particular points in the future; any dependencies with other events or changes; when you will call a halt to review progress and/or change plans
- **resources**: what the change is likely to cost (in broad terms).

Getting these factors clear at the earliest possible stage sets up a basic framework for planning change in further detail. Some factors may be 'immovable pillars' around which the more flexible aspects of change can be rearranged; others may be more adaptable.

Read more:

Ackoff's Best: His Classic Writings on Management

by Russell Ackoff

Players

Change is as much about people as it is about plans. Often, key individuals have the power to make or break a change effort through their support, indifference or opposition. So it's vital to get to grips with who these people are and how they are likely to affect the change.

First, list the players involved in change. Such individuals are sometimes termed 'constituents' or 'stakeholders'; whatever you call them, their defining characteristic is their interest in, or potential to be affected by, the change. You need to consider all the areas where players can be found, bearing in mind that some crucial players may be outside the business.

Internal players might include:

- **top management:** may need to change the decisions they take or how they take them, or adopt a new management style (see chapter 5)
- **middle management:** may have crucial roles to play in embedding the change (see chapter 5)
- **team leaders:** may be assigned tasks that are critical to the success of the change, or be in control of key resources
- **frontline staff:** may need to adopt new ways of working, or embody a new culture through the customer-facing part of the business
- **technical experts:** may have critical input into change planning, business continuity planning and the process of embedding change
- **culturally significant figures** (union reps, long-serving staff, respected managers, etc): may have a decisive influence over the way the change is perceived by others within the business.

External players might include:

- **customers:** may expect to be kept informed, or have unique insights into what needs changing

- **suppliers:** may be required to work in new ways, or meet new business requirements
- **partners and allies:** may be concerned about the effects of change on your relationship with them, or interested in the benefits that changes may bring them
- **shareholders:** may be concerned about the effects of changes on the value of the company
- **professional consultants** (accountants, management consultants, etc): may have their own views on what is best for the company or seek reassurance on the advisability or viability of change.

A full list of players could be very long indeed; you could make a case for almost anyone related to the business having some kind of interest. You will have to decide what constitutes a significant interest in change, or (to put it another way) one that it is worthwhile managing.

There may be players whose influence is outweighed by the effort required to manage it. You may decide that it is simply too much effort to get them involved, even though their contribution could be significant. Or it may be that their opposition, perhaps deeply entrenched, is so unlikely to change that you simply have to work round it. Take these decisions now, on rational business grounds, and try not to be swayed by personal pressures later on.

Having identified the players, pinpoint their interest in the change:

- **impact on work:** workload; prospects; pay and conditions; material loss or gain; new responsibilities; new issues to deal with; problems taken away
- **beliefs and attitudes:** what they feel about themselves, the business and their place in it (as far as you can tell)
- **personal motives and priorities:** likely emotional responses to the change, in particular any areas where they are likely to feel they are losing out; reasons for taking a particular attitude to change; outcomes they would like to see from change
- **personal history:** what past actions might have a bearing now (e.g. they had a hand in creating the current situation, or managed failed efforts to change in the past)
- **critical input:** what they have to do to make the change a success

- **likely level of support:** to what extent they will support or oppose the change and the reasons why this is so; whether they are simply neutral
- **active or passive:** whether support will be backed up by action or just kind words; whether opposition will take the form of inaction and foot-dragging or specific, active responses aimed at preventing change
- **capacity to help or hinder:** relationships (formal or informal), situations, strengths or attributes that make this person uniquely able to assist or resist the change.

Understanding these factors forms the foundation for overcoming resistance to change.

Recruiting key players

Once the players and their interests are identified, you can begin to think about who you want to be involved, what you will ask of them, and how you will recruit them.

Depending on the resistance to change within the business, achieving involvement may be relatively easy or a real uphill struggle. It may be a question of building an initial coalition of people who are committed to change, then seeking to strengthen it by recruiting others to the cause. In this kind of situation, it's worth considering the best sequence for recruiting supporters. Some individuals may have great value in helping recruit others; in fact, this may be the only contribution they make to change, but it's a crucial one.

The table overleaf shows some typical issues involved in recruiting players to the cause. The business in this fictional example is an automotive components distributor. It supplies products such as valves, filters, bearings and fastening devices to business customers. The sales department currently has salespeople assigned to product lines who get a commission based on the overall sales of their line.

The proposed change is the implementation of a customer relations management (CRM) system. This will involve a restructuring of the sales department from an organisation based on product lines to one based on customers. Each customer will have a designated account manager to understand their needs and co-ordinate all the supplies that they need. The new structure will reduce co-ordination headaches for the customer, since they will have just one point of contact for all the products they need. Salespeople will be rewarded with a commission plus a bonus based on customer satisfaction.

Three key figures need to be recruited, in the order shown in the table below, so that commitment can work its way up the organisation. As these three figures commit, many other individuals (perhaps those with no strong views either way) will become committed too.

There is more on the particular roles played by middle and senior managers in chapter 5.

Communicating the need for change

For change to gather momentum, people within the business have to understand the need for it. When a change is proposed, people focus on their own responsibilities, relationships and problems. Viewing a change from this perspective, they may not perceive the need for it.

A key first step, therefore, is to communicate the need for change in business terms, and relate that perspective to the personal sphere. People usually have a good idea of what they do and how it fits with the people and processes that are

Recruiting key players:

Player	Role
Marketing manager □ Frustrated with customer complaints; she has pushed for stronger customer focus in the past	**Change champion** □ She is strongly in favour and very unlikely to waver in her commitment. She therefore makes a good 'anchor' for the change effort
Deputy sales manager □ Young, ambitious and well regarded within his department; he wants to make his mark	**Middle manager** □ Well placed to translate the benefits into terms that salespeople can understand. Will help to smooth over the transitional period
Sales manager □ Deep connections to board members; strongly committed to existing sales structure	**Top manager** □ His buy-in is crucial. If he does not commit, other salespeople won't either

close to them. However, they may not know how their role fits into the bigger picture. If the big picture is changing, as it will when major changes are in the air, people need to understand this wider context so they can relate their own situation to it.

If possible, people should make an active choice to learn more and get involved in change. To do this, they need to know what managers know, so they can arrive at the conclusion that change is necessary themselves. Sometimes, business leaders evolve processes and attitudes that withhold information from 'the troops', partly to magnify their own perceived importance as those who are able to understand it and partly because of a sense that 'a little learning is a dangerous thing' or that 'knowledge is power'.

But once people have the power that comes from knowledge, they can use it to support change. It is a matter of trusting people to make the right choices. While appearing 'risky', this type of approach actually reduces the risks of change by getting commitment upfront. Coercing people into supporting change by insisting that it is necessary will not have this effect; any minor setbacks during the change will serve to confirm people's suspicions that change was never necessary in the first place.

Recruitment method	Outcome
Appeal to shared aims ☐ Appeal to desire for change; present change as a response to her concerns	☐ She explains who needs to be committed, and their likely attitudes to the change; recommends approach to deputy sales manager
Appeal to self-interest ☐ Present the proposed change in terms that stress the benefits to him. Emphasise how good a successful change will make him look	☐ He 'plants the seed' in the sales department and is ready to endorse the change when his boss, the sales manager, discusses it with him
Go over his head ☐ Find directors who are sympathetic to customer concerns; link change to directors' priorities	☐ Change gets discussed at director level – and the sales manager responds to concerns of those he respects

The main type of information that needs to be shared relates to commercial realities. Businesses often 'protect' their employees from seeing information of this kind, covering areas such as:

- **profit and loss** figures (and underlying trends)
- **competitor activity**; competitor performance figures
- evidence of shifting **customer** expectations
- **shareholder** expectations.

Some managers may assume that everyone in the business knows these things, but everyone has a different perspective depending on their priorities. Typically, managers will have a stronger focus on the medium- and long-term prospects than those responsible for day-to-day business processes. Those managing change need to make the right links between these processes and the ways in which they need to change.

Sharing the understanding that things must change shares the responsibility for making change happen. Once people understand the consequences of their own decisions for the business as a whole, they are more likely to make decisions that bring business benefit. Ensuring that this understanding is based on facts helps to prevent it from becoming a banal insistence that 'we're all in this together'. Without evidence to back it up, it becomes a call to action without justification.

Similarly, admitting that mistakes have been made in the past, and accepting responsibility for them (rather than spreading them across everyone in the business), may be an important first step towards getting everyone's buy-in.

Raising the heat

We saw in the previous chapter how it is sometimes necessary to disturb the equilibrium of an organisation, perhaps by creating a small team with a specific remit, so that new avenues for change can be identified. But what can be done if people just can't see any reason to move on from the way things are?

Raising the heat is about generating perceptions of the need to change. Often, this can be as difficult as actually making changes, but it's a vital first step in organisations where drivers for change are being ignored. As the name suggests, raising the heat is about emphasising the drivers for change, or expressing them in new ways, so as to create a sense of urgency and wake people up to the need for change. This leads to the perception that the current situation is untenable and that change is desirable, beneficial or even inevitable. In this new atmosphere, new directions will be welcomed rather than dismissed.

Some techniques include:

- **focusing on negatives** (or challenging tendencies to 'soft-pedal' them), such as:
  - financial losses; lower margins; falling turnover
  - loss of customers
  - low morale and/or negative perceptions of management within the business
  - poor public profile; declining or undesirable reputation
  - unfavourable changes in customer perceptions
- trying to bring the **unspoken assumptions** that support stability out into the open ('our market is not changing', for example); asking for evidence to support these beliefs
- considering **worst-case scenarios** as well as optimistic ones; questioning assumptions that worst-case scenarios cannot happen; pointing out any optimistic bias in projections
- discouraging **optimism based on past performance**; focusing on recent performance and/or actual current trends
- emphasising the **consequences of not changing**; questioning any hopeful assumptions that current negative trends will reverse themselves
- articulating **dissatisfaction with the status quo**; encouraging others to do so where possible
- emphasising the **benefits of changing** – the more definite, short-term, concrete and personally applicable these are, the better
- acknowledging the **possibility that change will fail**, while emphasising the probability of success and the necessity of at least attempting to change (aiming to pre-empt cynical dismissal of change efforts)
- **setting the tone through action**: taking tangible, visible steps that point towards the start of a change (cutting back on expense-account luxuries; circulating feedback from unhappy customers/ shareholders or information on competitors' strengths and recent successes, etc).

Real life : Raising the heat at Heineken

Dutch brewing giant Heineken has a long tradition of success, having been in the brewing industry for over 400 years. Although in third place globally in terms of size, it can claim to have the only global beer brand in the eponymous Heineken, recognised the world over in its distinctive green bottles.

For Heineken, success had been about building up a reliable brand in a stable marketplace, rather than radical upheavals. But by 2002/2003, drivers for change were all around:

- **poor performance**: earnings were flat, with stock trading at relatively low levels
- **changes in customer profile**: people today drink more wine; tougher drink-driving laws have led to changes in consumption patterns
- **competitor activity**: many new beer brands are entering the marketplace, many catering to niche interests and/or fads (e.g. low-carbohydrate)
- **outside factors**: weak global economy; the rainy summer in the USA in 2003; the SARS outbreak (which severely reduced social drinking in Asia).

The death of charismatic former chairman Alfred H. 'Freddy' Heineken in 2002 was hugely significant. Although canny in marketing terms, Freddy had been a brake on change in many ways, even after retiring in 1989. He resisted making expensive acquisitions, even though this allowed competitors to overtake Heineken through shrewd moves in this area. His impressive legacy, coupled with continued family involvement and ownership, means that change has been evolutionary rather than revolutionary, but his absence has meant more freedom to innovate.

Chief Executive Anthony Ruys had to make some tough decisions to move things forward. Bold acquisitions were one part of his strategy: during 2002, Ruys oversaw acquisitions costing a total of over £2 billion. Brewers were acquired from as far afield as Panama, Egypt and Kazakhstan, broadening the company's brand offering.

Getting into new market sectors was also vital. Ruys needed to instil a sense of urgency in Heineken's people. His tough approaches included producing a video for staff featuring a young Italian man saying 'I hate beer', the subtext being that 'safe', established brands like Heineken increasingly don't appeal to twentysomething drinkers, who regard them as tired and irrelevant.

The lessons that change managers can learn from Heineken include:

- **challenge assumptions**: for Heineken, years of dominance gave rise to the sense that success was a permanent attribute of the organisation, and this had to be challenged
- **share negative information**: old and/or family-run companies can be insular; people should not be shielded from bad results, or from what people are saying about the company
- **customer focus**: to find new directions, people at Heineken needed to get back in touch with what consumers really thought about their product and its place in the market
- **don't ignore culture**: in a long-established family firm, it may be advisable to present new directions as 'building on' past efforts, rather than a 'revolution'.

Note that much of this is focused on assumptions – the unspoken truths that lie behind many business decisions. Raising the heat is about bringing these into the open and getting them acknowledged. Those outside the normal loop of business (perhaps 'peripheral experts' from an informal network analysis – see chapter 5) can be helpful in bringing a more objective perspective to the beliefs and assumptions of a business. Someone who has seen what happened when similar businesses faced comparable issues might be invaluable.

Raising the heat has its hazards. There will still be those who deny the need for change in the face of all evidence – perhaps because they perceive that they will personally lose out when the changes come. Also, the person raising the heat needs to be fairly tough and resilient on a personal level – they will take the flak that is often directed at those who bring bad news. However, in organisations where stability has become institutionalised and reactive management is the norm, raising the heat can be the only way to move forward.

Persuasion

Convincing people to change can be a challenge. In the early stages, as we've seen, people's own priorities or frames of reference may make it difficult for them to see the need for change. Key players need to be recruited to the cause, not necessarily from an initial position of support. Later stages may involve making the case for resources to be allocated or structures to be transformed. At every stage, there is a good chance that people with make-or-break influence over the change will not be receptive to it. This makes persuasion a key change-management skill.

Management thinker Jay Conger has put forward some invaluable suggestions for those who have to persuade in business. Many of them challenge preconceptions about persuasion. Firstly, effective persuasion isn't about deceit or manipulation. It's about learning and negotiation: encouraging and enabling doubters to learn what you have learned, and leading them to an agreement.

The best persuaders can bring people round to a new way of thinking without seeming to 'win' and without the other party feeling that they have 'lost'. In change management, this is crucial. People often feel that they have much to lose through change.

Persuasion shouldn't be seen as a second-best or last-resort option, to be used when simply ordering people to do things has failed. Rather, it should be your first choice whenever there are potentially difficult issues to be resolved. Persuasion takes time and effort, but because it's based on understanding rather than coercion, it is ultimately more powerful.

Persuasion will also be vital if you are not in a position of authority but have nevertheless seen the need for change, and have to bring your superiors in the business round to your way of thinking.

Conger suggests four key components of persuasion:

- **establish credibility:** point to the expertise you have gained from your past experience to boost people's confidence in you
- **frame goals on common ground:** describe the benefits of changing in generally understood terms
- **vividly reinforce your position:** use examples, stories and metaphors for emotional impact
- **connect emotionally:** adjust your tone according to how receptive

your audience is; be ready for likely reactions and don't misjudge (or ignore) the mood.

He also identifies four big mistakes that would-be persuaders make:

- **trying the hard sell:** stating your position at the outset, then trying to drive it home through persistence, will have completely the wrong effect; by showing your hand early, you give people something to push against
- **resisting compromise:** compromise is not weakness or surrender; persuasion is about give and take; people want to see you demonstrate flexibility before they agree
- **focusing on the argument:** having a sound, defensible position is vital, but it's just one part of the equation; the four key components listed above are just as important
- **trying to complete the process too quickly:** persuasion is iterative and gradual, not a one-shot effort; a shared solution is unlikely to be found first time.

Read more:

Winning 'em Over

by Jay A. Conger

Looking back:

Key ideas from this chapter

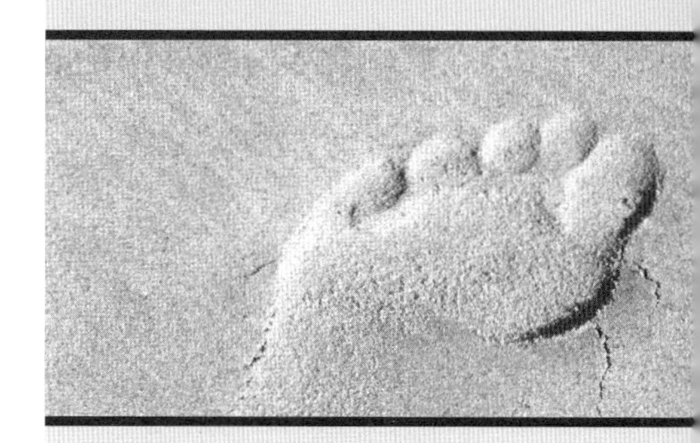

- Understand what you're aiming for before you start.
- Decide what's in and what's out.
- Identify the players; understand what drives them and how they will view the change; consider how and when to recruit them.
- Communicate the need for change and 'raise the heat' to achieve buy-in.
- Use persuasion to bring people around to the message of change.

4 Planning

This chapter covers the plans you should have in place before beginning a change effort.

Identify the options

There is usually more than one way to achieve a change goal. The first step in planning a change is to identify the different ways in which it could be achieved, and decide which one(s) will be taken forward.

To get this process started, define the options available in broad terms. You should aim for a small number of approaches that are substantively different from each other. How many options you consider depends largely on the resources you have available for managing change.

The big question here is 'what are the alternative ways of achieving the goal?' In other words, given the destination you have chosen, what different routes could you take to get there?

Each alternative then needs to be assessed in terms of its relative strengths, by considering questions such as:

- **business benefit:**
  - **quick wins:** short-term, visible benefits this option will bring
  - **long-term gains:** what this option will do for the business in the long term

- ☐ **cultural benefits:**
  - ☐ positive or desirable **messages** that choosing this option will send
  - ☐ positive **perceptions** that it will generate or reinforce
  - ☐ **desirable behaviours** that will be required, enabled or encouraged
  - ☐ **undesirable behaviours** that will be discouraged
- ☐ **strategic fit:**
  - ☐ what this option will do to **advance the business's central aims**
  - ☐ any potential this option has to **take the business off course** (a possible danger with quick wins)
  - ☐ whether this option has also been chosen by **competitors,** and if so, whether this is positive or negative
- ☐ **risks and uncertainty:**
  - ☐ **the probability of success** with this option
  - ☐ the **possibility of failure** with this option, and the implications (operational, financial, cultural, motivational, reputational, etc)
  - ☐ any obvious **potential problems** with this option; their likelihood and impact
- ☐ **possible 'process' problems:**
  - ☐ likely **timescale** for completing the change with this option
  - ☐ **resources required** (manpower, management time, investment, infrastructure, commitment)
  - ☐ **technical obstacles** (such as the requirement to source a new or unfamiliar technological solution)
- ☐ **possible 'people' problems:**
  - ☐ what the **objections** are likely to be
  - ☐ **who** is likely to object
  - ☐ the **reasons** for their objections
  - ☐ how these objections might be **countered**
- ☐ **key player implications:**
  - ☐ **dependencies** on any key players for success
  - ☐ specific **sacrifices or commitments** that key players will have to make
  - ☐ **benefits** for key players
  - ☐ **reliance** on particular individuals or relationships.

Considering these areas in relation to each option will help you decide which one is the best. The definition of 'best' depends on the change in prospect and the nature of your business, including its cultural values. For example, an option requiring significant resource may be less appealing to a small business. An option that involves significant changes in people's behaviour may be difficult to bring about in a large, highly traditional firm. However, such options may still be the best (or only) way to achieve the change that is required.

Don't put too much effort into debating small points of implementation or resource at this stage – one important aim here is to definitively rule out unrealistic options, so as not to waste any further time considering them. The realistic options can then be assessed in more detail, until the best one becomes clear.

Prioritisation

Within the overall change aim, there are likely to be subsidiary or component changes. It is critical to think about the order of these changes. Prioritisation can have a huge impact on the success of change.

Prioritising means considering questions such as:

- ☐ **dependencies:** what things must be changed before other things can change?
- ☐ **resource dependencies:** which changes will, once completed, free up or generate resources that will enable subsequent changes? are there any crucial change resources that will take a while to create or obtain?
- ☐ **strategic objectives:** what wider business aims does the change, or any part of it, need to fit in with?
- ☐ **technical or practical constraints:** are there any technical problems that need to be solved before change can proceed?
- ☐ **time constraints:** how long will each part of the change take? what are the implications of reordering changes for the overall timescale of change? are there other milestones that change has to harmonise with?
- ☐ **personal priorities:** what results do key players want to see? what issues do they want to see addressed as a condition of giving support to the change?
- ☐ **culture:** which changes will be easy because they're in tune with your business's culture? which changes will take more time and effort because they involve cultural change?

- **the need for quick wins:** are there any changes that will demonstrate, early on and in a tangible way, that change effort is having a positive effect? should they be prioritised – perhaps for this reason alone? would you trade off cost or effectiveness against a quick win? what will be the consequences of prioritising on 'rational' lines if this means there are no visible benefits from change for a long period?

Constraints and obstacles

Change planning must be rooted in reality. Many change efforts fail because those managing them are not realistic enough about the constraints and obstacles that threaten change.

Constraints and obstacles should be confronted explicitly, since problems – actual or anticipated – make good catalysts for resistance to change. Neglecting, ignoring or glossing over the difficulties involved in change is a gift to people who wish to dent the credibility of those proposing or managing change by implying that they do not know how the business really works, that they haven't thought through potential problems, or (perhaps most damaging) that they are attempting to push through change hastily against people's wishes.

To guard against this, acknowledge the potential for problems openly, at the earliest opportunity, and set out what you plan to do about them, with contingency plans if appropriate. This should be a key part of your communications with players and others about the change.

Practical or technical problems can be stated in simple terms. The description of cultural obstacles, and the solutions to them, may need to be expressed diplomatically to avoid damaging commitment to change.

Dimensions of agreement

In an ideal world, change planning would be based on an established consensus over the aims of change and the best options for achieving them. In the real world, there are always different perspectives on both.

Change plans will be affected by the level of agreement that can be achieved, and also the nature of this agreement, which has two dimensions: agreement over 'ends' (aims) and agreement over 'means' (options for implementation).

Even once players are recruited to the change cause (in other words, they agree about the aims of change), they may have very different opinions over the options for realising it.

The two dimensions of agreement are shown in the diagram below. The four quadrants reflect a simple division between high and low agreement in two dimensions; in practice, the situation is likely to be more complex. But this technique can help to indicate where efforts at persuasion or communication need to be concentrated.

If you feel your change is in the low/low quadrant, the prospects are not good. Not only do those involved not agree on how change should be achieved, they don't agree on what is being aimed for. Before planning can proceed, you need to define success – agree the outcomes that change will achieve – and then move on to look at options. It may be that you are obliged to proceed with change in this situation, but be aware that there are significant risks.

In the two low/high quadrants, you have some agreement to build on. The consensus can be expanded by identifying the core interests that everyone shares, and working to bring differing viewpoints closer. Here, it is a question of recruiting key players, using informal networks (covered in chapter 5) and

Dimensions of agreement:

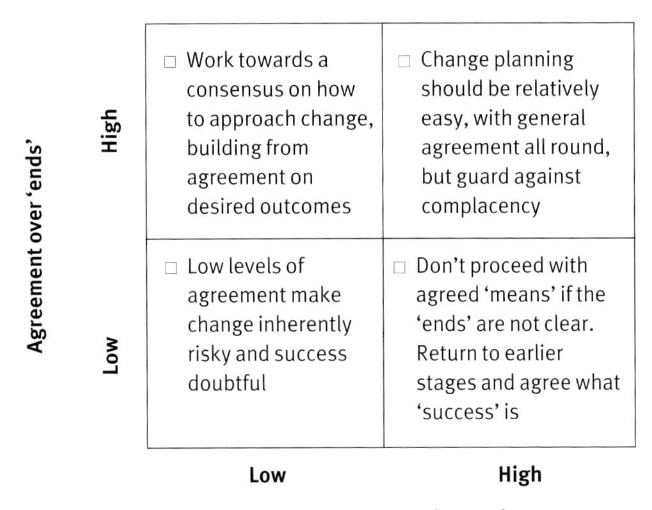

deploying persuasion skills to build up agreement in other areas. Discussing questions such as 'what do we all agree needs to change?' and 'what do we all agree will be effective?' may help.

Differences of opinion should be welcomed, since they provide the opportunity for creative, constructive discussion that can throw up new options. If there are no differences of opinion – that is, you are in the high/high quadrant – prospects for change are fair, but there is also the danger that there are better options that have not been explored. Without disagreement and discussion, these may never be discovered. Both ends and means should be questioned and analysed to ensure that they are really best for the business.

Set key milestones

Setting milestones is about deciding what will happen when. Closely linked to prioritisation, it is invaluable in getting to grips with complex and far-reaching changes to prevent them becoming open-ended, unfocused periods of undirected activity.

Milestones should be defined in terms of result and/or timescale. The effect is to divide up the planned change in terms of duration and component activities. The results need to be concrete, easily measurable and not open to subjective assessment (in other words, everyone will agree whether or not they've been achieved). For maximum certainty, set out and agree during the planning stage how your success in achieving a milestone will be measured.

So the key points to consider about milestones are:

- how much **time** will have elapsed, or what will have been **achieved**, or both
- **how you will tell** when the milestone has been reached
- **what you will do** when the milestone has been reached.

Reaching a milestone presents two important opportunities: the chance to celebrate and/or learn from your change efforts so far, and the chance to redirect the change effort if it is drifting off course. Change can bring new perspectives, and it may be that priorities or aims will need to change later on.

The cost of change

Change can be a costly process. It takes resources of many kinds, for example:

- **management time**: planning and managing the process; communicating the need for, and benefits from, change
- **opportunity cost**: time spent on change cannot be spent on 'real work'
- **consultancy costs**: outside help may be needed with any part of the process or its management
- **pilot schemes**: experimenting to see how change might work takes time and money
- **training**: new ways of working will need to be explained to the workforce.

An important part of planning change is assessing the resources that will need to be obtained, created or diverted in order to make change happen. Many changes fail because not enough effort is put into them, so this needs to be a realistic assessment. Your ideas on cost need to form part of the case for change. This can be very helpful in presenting change not as a wildly ambitious scheme or a personal interest that is being indulged, but rather as a logical, almost contractual exchange: 'if you spend this money, you should see this result'.

Being over-optimistic about cost may seem like a good short-term way to get change off the ground, but it can backfire. People may see through your positive estimates straight away, and this will damage commitment to change. Alternatively, estimates may be proved wrong in the fullness of time, in which case a successful change might be made to look like a failure. You need to create a situation where change efforts will be judged by the outcomes they have achieved, not their cost in terms of resources.

Destructive and creative change

Sometimes, the cost of change to a business is more than simply resources or finance. It's worth considering just how much has to change in order to achieve your aims, and what the true cost of profound change will be.

In recent years, much guidance on change has focused on 'creative destruction', or sweeping away everything that's gone before and putting something new in its place.

Characteristic approaches of 'creative destruction' changes include:

- getting rid of **functional teams**; creating new ones
- **centralisation or decentralisation** of key business functions
- **removing** entire organisational layers
- **outsourcing** key business functions.

Any of these might be less destructive if carried out gradually or incrementally, but it is characteristic of 'creative destruction' that changes of this nature are effected as quickly as possible, in a 'big bang' change. The idea is that a single, 'once and for all' transformation will allow the business to assume its ideal form. The process may be difficult, but the ends justify the means. Business Process Reengineering (BPR) was a technique for achieving this that became very popular during the 1990s.

The cost of creative destruction can be very high – not just resource-wise, but also in human terms. Transformational change can be a highly painful experience for everyone involved. It's also high-risk – by concentrating uncertainties into a short timeframe, it can maximise the chances of multiple problems cropping up faster than people can deal with them. The change process can end up being so traumatic that the business cannot recover – in other words, 'the operation was a success, but the patient died'. This is particularly true of smaller enterprises, where resources are limited and big change brings big risks.

The problems are often compounded through repetition – wearied by repeated (or simultaneous) change initiatives, people develop 'change fatigue', become cynical about change and drastically reduce their commitment to it.

As we saw in chapter 2, transformation is not the way in which living things achieve radical change. Gradual change, constant evolution and punctuated equilibrium can make big changes – not quickly, but with less trauma. Working with what you have can be just as viable as throwing it away and starting again.

Management thinker Eric Abrahamson suggests that when planning change, thinking in terms of 'creative recombination', or using the elements already present within the business to create something new, can be highly beneficial.

He divides the resources or elements of the business into five categories, each offering a different perspective on how change could be achieved without huge upheaval:

- **people:**
  - what **skills, talents and abilities** can people offer?
  - how could they be **redeployed**?
  - can **downsizing**, and its devastating impact on morale, be avoided?
- **informal networks** (see chapter 5):
  - what are the **networks** within the business?
  - what do they currently **achieve**, how and for whom?
  - how can they be made to work for the change rather than against it?
- **values and culture:**
  - what **attitudes** are generally held within the business that can be regarded as useful or positive (i.e. supportive of change)?
  - would it help the change effort to **restate**, reaffirm or rediscover them?
- **processes:**
  - what **approaches and systems** work well?
  - could they be **duplicated** elsewhere, or **redirected** to achieve other outcomes?
- **structures:**
  - what **teams**, relationships between teams, reporting arrangements, lines of communication and other structural systems work well?
  - can structure be **changed** without complete revision?

Read more:

Change Without Pain

by Eric Abrahamson

Contingency plans

In many situations, the actual outcome of change will not be certain, although the general aim may be clear. It is likely that a number of different outcomes will be possible. For example, a marketing drive may aim at increasing sales by 10%. Anything less than this might be regarded as failure, but of course any number of outcomes are possible.
Sales may increase by 5%, 7%, 9%, 12%, or any other figure.

The best-planned changes take account of the possible results of change and build in some contingency plans to be prepared for them.

Some typical contingencies for which you might need to plan are:

- **complete failure:** no business benefits whatsoever
- **partial success:** success in one part of the business only, or with one group of people only, or in one market sector only, etc
- **cost issues:** successful change, but costs higher than expected
- **timescale issues:** successful change, but takes longer than expected.

In order to plan for contingencies, you first need to define the actual outcome that each contingency refers to. You should already have defined success, but what constitutes 'failure'? What different outcomes between success and failure are possible? Is each one distinct, or are they points along a line?

You then need to understand two key attributes of each contingent outcome: its probability and its impact. How likely is it that the various possible outcomes will come about? And if they do, what will be the impact on the business?

Ideally, this analysis will be done using the techniques of risk management, which help you focus on probabilities, impacts and the results of decisions. For change, the key areas to concentrate on are:

- what are the different possible **outcomes** of change?
- what is the **probability** (likelihood) of each one happening?
- what would be the **impact** on the business if each one occurred?

Probability can be a highly subjective concept, involving translating our ideas about how likely different outcomes are into numerical terms. Change often deals with the unknown or unprecedented, and it can be extremely difficult to know what results our actions will have. But working towards a shared idea of probability allows us to compare the different possible outcomes in a more objective way, rather than falling back on terms such as 'fairly likely', 'less likely' and so on.

Impacts can affect any part of the business; the impacts of failure or partial failure are likely to be primarily in the areas that you are trying to change, but perhaps in other areas too. You need to consider what the business and cultural impacts of all the possible outcomes will be, and make plans to deal with those that are likely to happen and/or those that could have a significant impact.

Planning all this will take time and therefore could increase the cost of change. But demonstrating realism about the possibility of failure, coupled with concrete plans to deal with it, could help to build commitment to change. While you should always be aiming for success, it does no harm to cover your back at the same time.

Read more:

Risk: How to make decisions in an uncertain world

edited by Zeger Degraeve and Nigel Nicholson

The change team

Few changes can be effected by a single individual. Most significant changes will need a team to make them happen – not necessarily a full-time team that sits together in a room working on the change all day, every day, but a team bringing together the diverse skills that are required to make change a reality.

The key attributes of change teams are:

- they must represent **all relevant parts** of the business
- they must have sufficient **respect, authority and control** over resources to make change happen
- they must have the skills to **communicate** about their work with everyone they need to.

Note that these are attributes of the team as a whole, not any person within the team. In order to represent all relevant parts of the business, the change team may need to have a particular number of members. It's unlikely that a single person could represent the interests of everyone in a business, even in a very small organisation.

Richard Hackman, a leading researcher on groups, has identified five conditions for effective teams. It's easy to see how they link up with the requirements for a change team. These conditions are:

- **a real team**: one that has a specific task, a clearly defined and reasonably stable membership and clearly delimited authority (this links with defining success and deciding boundaries)

- ☐ **a compelling direction:** something to aim for (understanding the goal of change and the driving business reasons why it must happen)
- ☐ **an enabling team structure:** fostering motivation, creativity and learning; setting the right norms for conduct in the team; getting the composition of the team right
- ☐ **a supportive context:** rewards and recognition for the team's work; information (particularly on performance) to help planning and focus; education and training support
- ☐ **expert team coaching:** leadership intervention at the right time to pre-empt or troubleshoot problems.

Read more:

Leading Teams

by J. Richard Hackman

Looking back:

Key ideas from this chapter

- ☐ Consider all the options for how you can change and choose the most effective.
- ☐ Prioritise the changes you need to make.
- ☐ Acknowledge the constraints and obstacles affecting change; make contingency plans in case things go wrong.
- ☐ Set key milestones for the change.
- ☐ Assess the cost of change; consider what really needs to change and what the cost to the business in a wider sense might be.
- ☐ Make sure the change team has all the necessary skills.

5 Culture

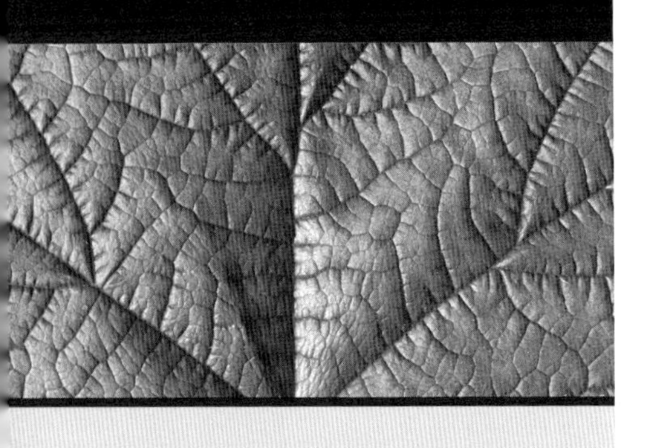

Planning is important, but change is more than a schedule or process. Business change happens in a living environment: as we've seen, businesses should be considered as living things with their own 'personalities', or cultures.

Just like other living things, businesses have their own personalities – their own cultures. Cultural issues are not secondary or optional considerations when planning change, to be considered as an afterthought; they should form an integral part of change management from the beginning. Crucially, culture often dictates the best way to overcome resistance to change in your business.

What is business culture?

Culture is the character of a business. It's 'they way we do things around here'. Culture affects how people relate to each other, work with each other and resolve problems in the workplace.

Culture exists in people's minds and the relationships that they form with their colleagues. We can't see these thoughts and relationships directly, but they find expression and manifestations in many familiar areas of business life:

- **values:** people's shared long-term goals and guiding principles that are embodied in business norms, practices and ways of viewing the world
- **unwritten rules, customs and conventions** (as opposed to their 'official' equivalents)

- **beliefs, perceptions and assumptions** (as opposed to positions based on fact)
- **informal networks** and power structures (as opposed to formal structures and hierarchies)
- **support networks**: how people help others with their problems outside work
- **rituals**: out-of-hours gatherings; social functions
- **workspace**: how space is shared, allocated and used; the way people's territories are defined and marked; corporate and personal decoration
- **communication**: how information is shared (conversation, meetings, email, memos, etc); what kind of information is shared (business or personal)
- **time management**: what people spend time doing; the hours they work; attitudes to long hours; the work/life balance
- **identity**: whether people identify with each other, their team, the business as a whole, or see themselves as individuals.

Culture is often most keenly and immediately felt by those visiting a business for the first time. Walking into a workplace and seeing the décor, the way desks are arranged, the level of noise or chat, people's body language and many other factors usually gives a strong sense of the culture of a business.

The fact that culture is essentially a mental or emotional phenomenon does not make it a weaker organisational force, or one that is somehow less relevant to management than 'harder' business issues – quite the reverse. The way we relate to each other as people at work can have a profound impact on our motivation to succeed, our desire to innovate and our drive to make changes. All of these are crucial to the future of the business.

Understanding your culture

Management writers Rob Goffee and Gareth Jones have devised a valuable framework for identifying different types of business culture, and deciding what might need to change.

To diagnose the kind of culture you have, you need to assess the levels of the 'two Ss' in your business:

- **sociability**: friendship; mutual support; sharing personal information; the workplace as a family

- **solidarity:** professionalism; mutual interests; working together; clear, shared goals.

Whether these 'Ss' are high or low within your business dictates, in very broad terms, what kind of culture it will have. No culture is inherently good or bad – each has its place – but each one has a positive and a negative form, depending on how the particular type of culture affects people and decision making within the business.

The four types of culture are shown in the table opposite. Although a first look suggests that the communal culture might be 'the best', each one can be appropriate in different circumstances. For example, newspaper reporters, academics and researchers often need individual freedoms to do well, and so may thrive in a fragmented culture. A mercenary culture, while often a tough place to work, may be right for those who like to focus on results rather than friendships; finance houses often create this kind of high-pressure environment, and those who work there either enjoy it or decide they can live with it.

Often, a business will not be characterised by a single culture; teams or departments within it may show different tendencies; for example, a communal 'cell' may arise within a culture that is networked overall. This is one reason why small teams can be such a powerful force for change, as we saw in chapter 2.

Over time, businesses can 'slip' from the positive to the negative form of a particular type, or from one type to another. For example, when people drift apart or have less reason to work together in a networked culture, it will gradually become a fragmented culture.

It is relatively easy to prevent the slip from positive to negative if proactive efforts are made to manage culture. As we've seen, growth presents particular challenges, and culture is one area where growth can lead to change and present the need for culture to be actively managed.

Changing a culture is extremely difficult – far more so than restructuring or re-engineering a business. But in some circumstances there is no other way to move forward, if culture is preventing growth or development.

Read more:

The Character of a Corporation

by Rob Goffee and Gareth Jones

Types of culture:

Type	Character traits	In positive form	In negative form
Networked (high sociability, low solidarity)	□ participation □ friendships and networking □ networking throughout the organisation □ helping others	□ relaxed, informal, flexible and supportive environment □ high levels of trust, empathy and care for others □ loyalty; no hidden agendas	□ can be tolerant of poor performance □ gossip, rumour and politics □ long meetings with nothing agreed
Mercenary (low sociability, high solidarity)	□ performance and effectiveness □ hard work □ material reward □ destroying the competition	□ focused, task-oriented □ good awareness of competition □ recognition of shared interests □ intolerance of poor performance; focus on improvement	□ lack of co-operation □ people only do what is measured □ poor at exploring opportunities for synergy and alliances
Fragmented (low sociability, low solidarity)	□ people working alone □ few links with colleagues □ aiming for goals outside the organisation	□ freedom from interference □ scope for individual creativity □ individuals set own goals and agenda □ resources go to those individuals who can deliver	□ selfish and secretive □ new ideas savaged □ meetings and collective events difficult to manage □ people don't identify with the business
Communal (high sociability, high solidarity)	□ deep friendships □ shared values of sociability □ family atmosphere □ a passion for the business and what it does □ sense of value in work	□ passionate and committed □ high-energy, creative and stimulating □ close tie between values and practices □ loyal, fair and equitable	□ sense of invulnerability; inability to see strengths of competitors □ reliance on charismatic founders □ confusing positive beliefs with good performance □ unwillingness to change

Real life : Changing the culture of the BBC

When Greg Dyke, Director-General of the BBC, resigned in the wake of the Hutton Inquiry, staff at BBC offices around the country went outside their workplaces to protest. Many were in tears. All expressed heartfelt support for Dyke and the position in which he found himself. What kind of manager inspires such emotion?

When Dyke took over the BBC in 1999, there were plenty of external drivers for change. Commercial stations were eroding the BBC's market share, and questions were being asked about its place in modern broadcasting. These drivers remain in force today, but a big part of the BBC's problem in the late 90s was the effect they were having on its culture. From a communal culture, with a strong sense of shared mission, the BBC had become fragmented. Departments and functions were in conflict: radio and TV, sport and entertainment, programme makers and commissioners all had grievances against each other, and issues were kicked about in a culture of blame. Everyone felt under attack; no one dared to be innovative.

Greg Dyke made many 'hard' business changes at the BBC. He reduced overheads from 24% of revenues to 15% inside five years, drastically cut spending on consultants and reorganised support functions. These changes brought benefits, but they were just part of a bigger change project: improving the culture of the BBC.

The key points of Dyke's cultural change were:

- **trust/no blame:** respect for other people's ideas was paramount; yellow cards bearing the words 'Cut the crap: make it happen' were handed to those who scorned others' ideas in meetings; trust was encouraged
- **changing structure to change culture:** an entire organisational layer was removed, to bring programme makers closer to broadcasters and producers; programme makers were given places on the BBC's Executive Committee
- **openness:** meetings became more informal; new ideas and involvement were encouraged; Dyke discouraged politics by dealing with issues in group settings, not one-on-one
- **communication:** reporting became simpler and more direct; Dyke sent personal emails to staff explaining precisely what he wanted from them
- **collaboration:** the Executive Committee became a forum to discuss themes that affected different divisions within the organisation

- **self-reliance and self-responsibility:** Dyke encouraged all staff to feel that they could change things, and that it was up to them to do so
- **emotional connection:** Dyke's warm and friendly personal style distanced him from 'the old guard' and made people want to work for him
- **active management of culture:** social events and other functions helped to recreate the communal culture that had been eroded.

BBC staff liked what they saw, and new initiatives started to happen – many of them suggested by BBC staff who were encouraged to contribute. Dyke's cultural change reaped real business benefits by re-establishing a feeling of belonging, shared goals and real achievement. Not even the verdict of the Hutton Inquiry could dent the legacy of his leadership within the BBC.

Read more:

Leadership and the Psychology of Turnarounds

by Rosabeth Moss Kanter

Ways to change culture

It is the mark of a mature organisation that it is conscious of culture and realises that it needs active management.

The first step is to identify the culture. But achieving agreement on this may not be straightforward. In some businesses, and particularly long-established ones, there can be a divergence between the reality of culture and its public face. For example, managers may have one idea of culture, while others have a very different perception.

Having identified the kind of culture you have, or worked through the various perceptions of it, you need to decide whether it is the kind of culture you need. Your culture may have evolved in response to factors that are no longer as relevant as they were:

- the **personality of the business's founder**, even though they may be long retired
- **market conditions** that are no longer extant
- **social values** and **customer preferences** that have since changed
- **management structures** that are no longer right for the business.

You cannot enforce a cultural change. Cultures exist in people's heads, so they are difficult or impossible to change directly. But there are things you can do to enable or promote change. First, identify the reasons why culture is the way it is, and question whether it still needs to be so – raise the heat for cultural change. Then consider what practical steps could be taken that might encourage cultural change to follow. Some possible areas to focus on are:

- **rules and policies:** get rid of those that hinder the change; create new ones that support it
- **goals and measurement:** set goals that are linked to change objectives
- **customs and norms:** actively create new customs that support the change (for example, switching from memos to meetings as the default mode of communication)
- **training:** orient training plans to the change; deliver training 'just in time' so people can put it into practice straight away; provide 'hands-on' rather than theoretical training wherever possible

- **ceremonies and events:** establish new ones that reinforce new ways of working (giving awards and recognition, outings aimed at building sociability, etc)
- **management behaviours:** reward managers on the basis of how well they adapt to and embody new behaviours
- **rewards and recognition:** link rewards to achieving the goals of change
- **communications:** communicate in new ways to emphasise commitment to change; establish two-way communication
- **physical environment:** make a visible, tangible change to the environment to reinforce business change
- **structure:** set up teams, combine departments and eliminate or create management layers to reinforce the change.
- **selection:** changing the profile of employees by selection and de-selection

Read more:

Connecting Culture to Organisational Change

by Timothy Galpin

The informal network

The informal network is the reality behind the company structure chart: the network of informal relationships that makes things happen in the business.

Often, informal networks look very different from official structures. There may be individuals without great formal authority who nevertheless wield huge influence over the business. Conversely, there may be official authorities or managers whose real-world influence is negligible.

Knowledge of informal networks is likely to be subconscious, or not perceived as being linked to the 'real' business of the organisation. Knowledge of the informal network is also unlikely to rest with a single individual whom you can interview to get a 'snapshot' (people all have different perspectives anyway); getting an idea of informal networks involves a combination of observation, questioning and intuition.

To understand informal networks, you can look at a range of types of interaction:

- **information flows:**
  - who talks to whom?
  - what do they talk about?
  - why do they talk to each other?
  - what do they gain from the interaction? what is the unique appeal of the relationship for those involved? (For example, technical information, advance notice of business developments, useful advice, gossip and rumour, etc)
- **trust:**
  - who trusts whom, and why?
  - which events or situations have established trust?
  - does trust flow from 'real' work situations, or does it sometimes originate in purely social relationships?
  - who is trusted to safeguard the interests of specific individuals or groups?
  - is trust demanded or implicit?
- **respect:**
  - who has people's respect?
  - who are they respected by?
  - why are they given respect? (reasons may include ability, knowledge, decisiveness, experience, attitudes, temperament, long service, etc)
- **innovation:**
  - who gets together to discuss new ideas?
  - who is consistently innovative, occasionally innovative, never innovative?
- **decision making:**
  - who makes decisions?
  - are decisions made by individuals or groups?
  - is there a 'real' decision maker behind the 'official' decision maker?
- **energy:**
  - who energises people through their interactions with them?
  - who has a negative impact on people's energy?

By looking at these factors across a group, you can build up a picture of its informal network. A fictional network is shown on the diagram opposite. Each circle represents an individual, each arrow a relationship. In this diagram, the arrows denote simple 'working relationships' based on common goals, shared information, trust and respect. It may be helpful to specify the nature of the links between individuals, for example to discern where trust networks are at odds with formal authority.

Michelle and Dan are central connectors. They might be managers or just popular figures in the workplace (or both). Whatever the reason, they are central contact points for groups of people who might not otherwise interact with each other. Central connectors can use their influence to generate commitment to change.

Steve is a boundary spanner. He has links with the two central connectors, who are not in direct contact with each other. He has power over what information passes from one side of the network to another. His absence would have a huge impact on the way these two groups interact. He would be a key contact for understanding the full implications of a change that affected the whole network, and for ensuring that information about the change reached everyone involved.

Chris is a peripheral specialist. He isn't part of the network (he may be a consultant or freelance worker) but his knowledge is useful to people within it, and they turn to him for advice. It will raise the heat and emphasise the need for change

An informal network:

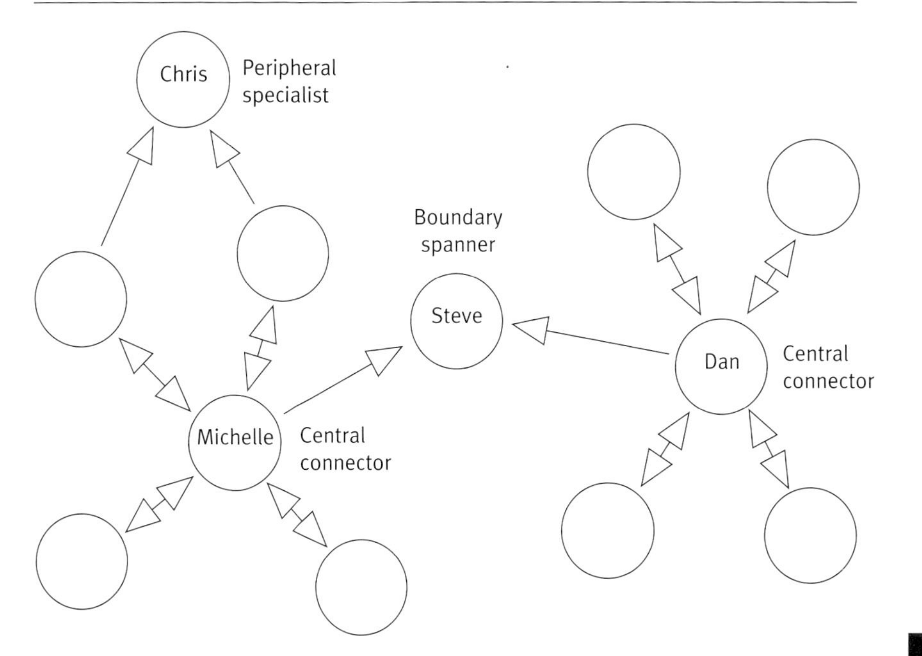

if his authoritative opinions are in line with the change goal, so that when people consult him he gives advice (or just general chit-chat) that supports, endorses or encourages the change.

It's important to note that much of Chris's value to the network comes from the fact that he is outside it. He has a fairly objective view of the business's strengths and weaknesses; he can provide a reality check to those inside it who find it hard to take a balanced view. Also, he probably deals with a number of businesses, so he can bring learning from other areas that in-house staff can't access. Trying to get this kind of value from Chris on a day-to-day basis by giving him a job might be a mistake – by joining, he leaves behind much of the perspective that makes him so valuable.

Management consultants are classic peripheral specialists in terms of their technical knowledge, but anyone can have a peripheral effect on the culture of the business. Indeed, those on the periphery may be able to affect culture very strongly. A senior figure who has left the organisation, perhaps for a competitor, but retains social links with certain staff would be an example.

People may have different views of informal networks; the more emotionally charged the interactions, the more likely they are to be perceived differently by different people. For example, a network built on sharing information will probably 'look' the same to all its members – people either have knowledge or they don't. But people may have widely differing views of who trusts whom (and who trusts them).

Read more:

The People Who Make Organisations Go – or Stop

by Rob Cross and Laurence Prusak

The role of top management

The commitment of those at the top of the business to the change is a crucial factor for success. As the people identified with setting direction and making decisions, and also often identified most closely with the values of the organisation, top management need to make their support clear through the change process. The credibility of change initiatives can be fragile, and a lack of commitment from the top (or even the suspicion of it) is often enough to derail a change.

To make change work, top management need to:

- acknowledge the **reasons** for change
- make an explicit, public **commitment** to change (not just tacitly or passively accept it)
- agree between themselves on the **aim** of change (the 'ends')
- in a broad sense, agree between themselves on **key tasks and projects**, timescales, resources (the 'means')
- ensure that they give out consistent, clear **messages** supporting the change
- keep control of **information** about the change
- **lead by example**, embracing change early and demonstrating commitment through actions as well as words.

Leading by example is a powerful motivator. For example, if new systems are introduced and presented as something that 'everyone' has to use and get accustomed to, it's important that 'everyone' is seen to include senior managers. This enhances the sense of change as something that is participative and shared, rather than unilateral and imposed, and is likely to help generate more commitment.

Where several managers are involved in a change initiative, achieving consensus may be difficult. This is particularly likely when a change initiative cuts across different departments or business areas that may have differing or even opposing objectives. There is a danger of the various managers arriving at a mutually agreed 'lowest common denominator' way forward that dilutes the aims of the change by including only the most conservative and cautious options.

Ideally, change should be publicly led or endorsed by a single senior figure (a 'change champion') or a coalition of managers. The number of managers required, and their actual positions, will vary according to the business (and its informal network); the key is that there must be enough managers on board for the change to achieve a momentum of its own. Managers who are inclined to be cynical need to be denied any opportunity to dismiss the change as irrelevant or portray it as a side issue not related to 'real' business. Getting their management colleagues on side at the earliest stage can help with this.

The role of middle management

Middle managers can be defined as those two levels below top management, or two levels above operational staff. They are often unfairly characterised as dull, unambitious time-servers who are likely to resist change rather than assist it. But not everyone can be a star. There are those who value the company as a whole more than their own careers as individuals, or who have certain work/life balances that they wish to preserve, or who simply prefer stability to constant transformation. Such people are likely to feel comfortable remaining in a middle management role rather than pushing for more responsibility.

Middle managers can play a key role in change – not necessarily by initiating changes and having innovative ideas (although they may well do so), but by helping to make change happen on a practical level and ensure that it becomes part of the everyday fabric of the organisation.

Middle managers can help change by playing four key roles:

- **entrepreneurs**: they are close enough to the 'sharp end' to spot problems, but also well positioned to appreciate the bigger picture
- **communicators**: they have strong credibility and understand informal networks; they can generate commitment to change without arousing suspicion or making people feeling threatened
- **therapists**: they can help with people's emotional needs during change; they can provide detailed one-on-one support and help with problems
- **'tightrope artists'**: they keep the business running smoothly through the change process, balancing the need for radical change with the necessity for continuity.

Not every middle manager will be able to do all these things; capabilities will vary from individual to individual and will depend on attitudes and experience. The middle managers most likely to make useful contributions during change are those who:

- are **eager to take part** in change initiatives
- **spot problems** with change plans and suggest solutions
- are **sought out** by others for advice and help
- have shown themselves to be **versatile and adaptable** during past changes.

Read more:

In Praise of Middle Managers

by Quy Nguyen Huy

Looking back:

Key ideas from this chapter

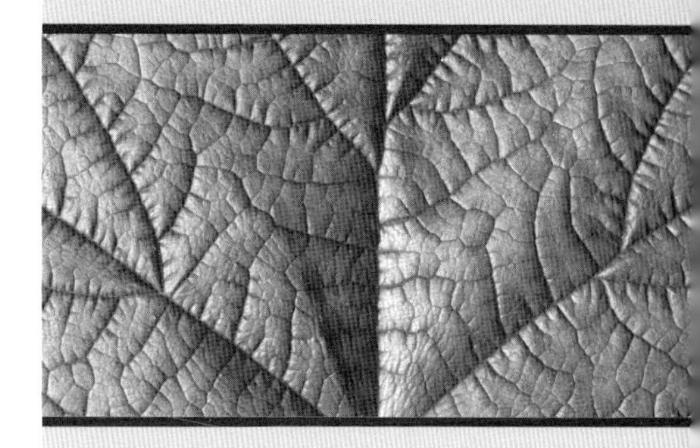

- Make sure you understand the culture of your business.
- Identify areas where cultural change is necessary, and consider how you can bring it about.
- Analyse the informal networks behind official structures.
- Decide what you will need from top management and middle management in order for change to succeed.

6 Communication

Communication is a central part of good change management. This isn't just about imparting information – it's about achieving involvement and commitment to the change, which is the key to breaking down resistance.

The importance of communication

Failing to communicate is a common factor in failed change efforts. It's not enough for those in charge of change to understand and deal with the various issues covered in this book so far. For change to work, people need to 'buy in' to it, and the key to this is knowledge. Although there may sometimes be reasons why information needs to be restricted, the principle that everyone should know what managers know is a good place to start when planning communication.

Those involved in managing change often underestimate the effort required to make this a reality. Wherever people go for information, they need to find messages that support change, and this will require a sustained effort to manage all the diverse information flows – formal and informal – that exist within the business.

Some principles of successful communication are:

- be **honest**; people aren't stupid
- if **difficult times** are ahead, apologise for bad news, but remember people want to hear

things straight; don't invoke 'the greater good' to those likely to lose out

- give people **time and space** to absorb and internalise the implications of, and need for, change; try not to backtrack on key points in response to criticism or dismay; let the message sink in for a while before returning with more information and/or reassurance
- stress the **benefits** of change clearly and realistically; communicate quick wins as soon as they occur; celebrate success and praise those who make change happen
- genuinely **listen** to what is said; be honest about what you cannot change, consider acting on what you can change
- remember that communication is a **two-way process**; face-to-face communication is ideal (one-on-one meetings, seminars, team meetings, any opportunity for consultation and interaction)
- don't worry about **overdoing it** – most change is characterised by lack of communication; repetition adds strength to the message and demonstrates commitment.

Involvement

The aim of communication should be to achieve the involvement of as many people as possible in the change effort. People do not resist their own ideas. By involving them in the process of making decisions about change, you can secure their active commitment to change, or at least make it less likely that they will resist it. The more people that can be involved in change, the greater the chance of success. The ideal is total involvement for total commitment and total success, but in reality this is unlikely to be possible.

Without involvement in change, negative perceptions can arise (whether they are true or not), such as:

- change is being **imposed** from above
- people's **opinions are not valued** by management
- people **cannot be trusted** to understand and discuss change
- management are **withholding information** because they are afraid of the reactions to change.

Real life : Involvement at Asda

The Asda supermarket chain was one of the most successful retail companies in the United Kingdom during the 80s, but by 1991 it had serious problems. Strategic direction was unclear, people lacked motivation, profits were declining and debts were increasing. Asda was facing bankruptcy.

New CEO Archie Norman's approach was characterised by bold leadership and a simultaneous emphasis on involvement. While he gave strong direction from above, steadying the ship and plotting a course for new horizons, he gained commitment from people within Asda by empowering them in new ways and making them feel part of the company's success.

Some of his techniques were:

- **communication**: a 'Tell Archie' programme encouraged people to come forward with issues and new ideas
- **acknowledging and managing culture**: in his first speech to executives, Norman stated that Asda needed 'a culture built around common ideas and goals that include listening, learning and speed of response'

- **disturbing the equilibrium using small teams**: 'risk-free' stores were set up, where people were encouraged to experiment without fear of being punished for failure
- **ensuring involvement**: rather than just talking about commitment, Norman appointed Allan Leighton – regarded as warmer and more of a 'people person' – to actually make it happen in the business
- **focusing on the sharp end**: Norman put a strong emphasis on the importance of Asda's stores – the 'sharp end' of its operation – as a focus for change: 'I want everyone to be close to the stores ... that is our business'.

Archie Norman's change programme wasn't just about 'soft' factors. Early on in his time at Asda, employees were laid off, wages were frozen and the company's structure 'flattened' – all with the explicit aim of increasing shareholder value. But because Norman had achieved a level of staff involvement, these changes did not generate the atmosphere of distrust that they might have done if they had been brutally imposed on the business.

Read more:

Cracking the Code of Change

by Michael Beer and Nitin Nohria

Very often, it is often these perceptions, rather than the actual aim of the changes, that prompt resistance.

By achieving involvement, you can create positive perceptions, including:

- change is a **collective effort**
- **opinions are valued** and acted on
- everyone in the business is **intelligent** enough to understand the case for change and help to create a solution
- **anyone** in the business would do the same thing if they were in a management position.

Not everyone can be involved at the same level, but any involvement will help. Aim to involve people at the level where they can add most value to the change.

A key question is how soon to involve people. We saw in chapter 3 how players need to be recruited in a particular order. For involvement to become a reality, everyone affected by the change needs to be considered as a 'player', in that they need to have some influence on the change. The timescale for this, and the order in which people are involved, needs to be carefully considered. On a practical level, there will be a need to balance the timescale and cost implications of consulting people and listening to what they say with the need to press ahead with change.

Sometimes, it is better to involve people on a practical rather than a planning level. Involvement in action can be more productive than involvement in discussion. Actions have a real-world effect and cannot be discounted as easily as opinions; contributing to (say) a quick win once change begins might actually generate more commitment in some people than being involved in lengthy discussions beforehand.

There will be situations where it's simply not possible to gain commitment or involvement. Any change that is clearly not in the interests of a particular group – such as redundancies – may be better made unilaterally and rapidly rather than through consensus. You can only achieve involvement on the basis of personal interest and benefit in the change; some changes simply don't allow this to happen. Hopefully, more positive changes in the future will be made on a basis of involvement.

Resistance

We have seen how important change is to businesses. But when change is proposed, people often resist it. There are several reasons, many sharing a common theme of divergence between organisational priorities and personal perspectives:

- **fear of the unknown:** there is a lack of concrete information about the change or its consequences; the future is not clear; there is uncertainty over the outcome of change
- **sense of threat:** people think (or assume) that the change will bring negative personal consequences (loss of status or privilege, changes to working patterns, new responsibilities)
- **no sense of urgency:** not understanding the reasons for change, or the ultimate individual consequences of the business failing to change
- **bad cultural fit:** the change is counter-cultural; it is not in harmony with 'the way we do things here', and therefore seems alien and threatening
- **bad structural fit:** the change is not aligned with existing structures, or will cut across them, or disrupt existing teams

- ☐ **lack of involvement:** people feel no commitment to the change because they have not been involved in decisions
- ☐ **change fatigue:** people have lived through repeated, failed efforts to change and have become cynics or prey to the BOHICA syndrome ('bend over, here it comes again').

Some tactics for overcoming resistance include:

- ☐ **acknowledge past change efforts:** learn from them and show that you've learned from them
- ☐ **acknowledge 'fixes that didn't work':** accept (and perhaps apologise for) past short-term fixes and other actions that did not address causes, only symptoms
- ☐ express changes as **building on past efforts** rather than sweeping them aside, to avoid implicit criticism of those who created the present situation
- ☐ focus on **commercial realities** (financial performance, competitor information, changing markets) to keep up the 'heat'; translate these into the ultimate personal consequences of the business not changing
- ☐ consider **players** who are likely resistors and their power to hold back change; start working on prominent doubters early, get them 'on side' so that others who sympathise with them will follow
- ☐ allow resistors to **express their views** in full, then deal with them; don't attempt to suppress resistance; allow people to let off steam before you start building a response; change may draw out old frustrations and resentments
- ☐ look for signs of **passive** resistance as well as active (withholding of effort or support, foot-dragging, distortion of key messages, unhelpful gossip and rumour)
- ☐ emphasise the importance of **different viewpoints** in shaping change
- ☐ emphasise the strong position at a later stage of those who **assist** change, or the rewards they may receive
- ☐ consider what **personal benefits** need to be offered: focus on what is being added to people's working life (security, better culture, etc), rather than what they are 'losing' through change.

What do people want to hear?

In all communication efforts, remember that the personal perspective is paramount. The key to communication about change is making a strong link between individual interests and group or business interests. For change managers, it is the group interests that come first. But for those hearing change messages, their individual interests come first. Consider what people want to know (what, why, what's the end result, what does it mean for me?) before what you want to say to them, and shape your communications accordingly.

People often have very different communication needs, based on their own character. Some will want facts and figures to be convinced of the need for change; the 'horizons' of their responsibility or interest will dictate the nature and extent of the data they need. The source of the information – an authoritative and unbiased third party, for example – may be important.

Others will just want to be 'stroked' by being offered reassurance that certain things will not change, that their status is unchanged, and their position is not under threat. Others may want both. For some, a single conversation may be enough; for others, it may be necessary to let messages sink in and deal with questions later. An iterative process, whereby details are gradually built up, may be required.

At the most basic level, people's communication needs are an expression of what is important to them. Once you are in touch with any insecurities or fears they have, you are halfway to creating the message that they want to hear.

Communication media

The table opposite shows some different media for communicating about change, with pros and cons listed for each. The main criterion for choosing one should be the preference of the recipient or participant, rather than the preferences of change managers. It's also important to consider which media are right for different kinds of communication. Written media get a lot of detail across, but generate little involvement. Face-to-face communications can generate much more involvement and sense of community, but may not be the most effective way to get information across. The best approach may be to use a range of media, each carrying variations on the same message.

The human animal

We saw in the last chapter how important informal networks can be in change management. Some managers may see informal networks as a problem to be worked around, or an undesirable phenomenon that should be stamped out, but this is naïve. Informal networks will spring up whenever a group of people come together, for whatever purpose.

Humans are social animals. In prehistoric times we banded together in order to maximise our chances of survival. The first human communities were characterised by almost continuous face-to-face interaction and bonds of close acquaintance, if not kinship. As a result, many of our mental strengths are intuitive and emotional rather than rational and structural. But the structures and processes we have developed in business often go

Communication media:

Medium	Benefits	Problems
Written media (web, email, newsletters)	☐ Precise ☐ Unambiguous ☐ Concrete and objective ☐ Get lots of information across	☐ Impersonal ☐ One-way
Presentations	☐ Communal ☐ Informal ☐ Memorable ☐ Some scope for dialogue	☐ Largely one-way
One-on-one meetings	☐ Personal ☐ Supportive ☐ Genuinely two-way ☐ Gauge reaction directly ☐ Address concerns directly and immediately	☐ Time-consuming ☐ Labour-intensive
Larger meetings (brainstorming, troubleshooting, etc)	☐ Hear lots of views ☐ Allow space for concerns to be aired and worked through	☐ Gives resistors a forum in which to 'gang up' on those managing change

against the grain of human nature. This can lead to tension between what managers want people to do, and people's underlying need to interact in the ways they have done for thousands of years.

The enlightened approach is to go with the flow. The most effective (and popular) change managers are those who aim to work with human nature, rather than against it. People will not resist change if they understand that it benefits the groups that they value, and the message of change is delivered through channels they like, by people they respect.

Other implications for change management include:

- **small teams work:** the structure of small 'families' (teams) organised into a 'village' (business unit or company) of not more than 150 people seems to be the most 'natural'; this is why small teams can be so effective in finding new directions while remaining valued by the larger group
- **status perceptions are crucial:** informal networks let us examine and re-affirm our status through means such as gossiping and telling stories; be mindful of the deep-seated need for status reassurance during change
- **face-to-face communication is best:** managers and employees generally like face-to-face communication best of all; it comes naturally to us in a way that reading and writing do not
- **people like stories:** remember that gossip – improvised news – will fill any gaps in communication; a plausible story will supplant complex or ambiguous facts; compelling narratives can be powerful tools in shaping attitudes
- **change has limits:** remember that however compelling or elevated the vision for change, it has to be put into practice by humans; our self-centredness will always influence and limit what we can achieve through change.

Read more:

Managing the Human Animal

by Nigel Nicholson

Vision

A vision is an idea of the future that acts as a focal point for all change efforts. Vision is about having a picture of the changed organisation as it will be when change has been successful: a sense of 'how it looks when it works'.

To be an effective tool, vision has to have substance. It should not be a management fantasy, slogan or platitude. Good visions function as useful guides and inspiration to those who have to make changes happen. They help to cut through doubts and details by getting to the heart of whether any particular project or action is the right one – does it contribute to realising our vision? If not, should it proceed?

Detailed change plans may affect many different areas of the organisation. As a result, they may not be understandable to everyone. But a good vision is clear and intelligible to everyone in the business, giving them a common goal to work towards. Just as change aims need to be articulated in a common language so that everyone understands the need for change, vision needs to express the desired future in a universally comprehensible way.

If you choose to use a vision statement as a means to focus change efforts, it's vital that it gets communicated to everyone. Management thinker John Kotter has identified seven keys to communicating a vision of change:

- ☐ keep it **simple** so that everyone can understand
- ☐ use **metaphors** to clarify change concepts (see 'mind pictures' below)
- ☐ use many **different media** to get the message across
- ☐ **repeat** the message to reinforce it
- ☐ **lead by example**; do not act in a way that is inconsistent with the vision
- ☐ **address perceived inconsistencies** between vision and action
- ☐ make communications **two-way**.

Read more:

Leading Change

by John P. Kotter

Real life : A compelling vision for the ANC

The African National Congress was originally founded in 1912 as a reaction to laws and taxes aimed at keeping black workers in low-paid jobs and curtailing their rights. Over the 80 years that followed, social and political drivers for change saw it transform itself into a mass movement opposing the racist oppression and discriminatory policies of the apartheid government in South Africa.

By the 1960s, it had become clear to the ANC that peaceful protest would not bring about change, and it resolved to take up arms against the government. Banned and suppressed, it went underground to try and further the 'armed struggle'. In mainstream South African society, the fight for liberation found expression through spontaneous strikes and student demonstrations. The momentum for change grew, and by the late 80s, civil unrest and disobedience were destabilising the apartheid regime. The government responded as it always had, with violent oppression, but by 1990 it could hold back the tide no longer. The ban on the ANC was lifted, and after 27 years in captivity, Nelson Mandela became president of South Africa in 1991.

Writing in his autobiography about the ANC annual conference of July 1991 – the first within South Africa for 30 years – Mandela describes the scale of the change facing the ANC at this time. 'For 30 years the ANC had functioned clandestinely in South Africa; those habits and techniques were deeply ingrained. We had to reconstruct an entire organisation, from the smallest local branch to the National Executive. And we had to do so in a matter of months during a period of extraordinary change ... In the new ANC, we had to integrate not only many different groups, but many different points of view.'

Mandela's opening speech to the conference included these words. 'It is our movement that has the vision, the policies, the programmes and the mature leadership which will take our country from its apartheid past to its democratic future. From this conference we must formulate the strategies and provide the leadership that can and will enable us to lead all the people of South Africa to the goal which the overwhelming majority seeks, that of justice, democracy, peace and prosperity.' He went on to spell out the practical and political challenges that lay ahead for the ANC in making this vision a reality.

Mandela's leadership and self-sacrifice have inspired people around the world. We can't compare his lifelong struggle against apartheid with management issues. But his words, here and elsewhere, illustrate the qualities that make good vision statements compelling:

- ☐ **simplicity**: easy for everyone to understand; not expressed in group-specific terms or jargon; as resonant for those outside the organisation as those within it
- ☐ **clear goals**: the key aims – for the conference and beyond – are set out simply and concisely
- ☐ **inclusiveness**: involving everyone in change; avoiding blame for the past; seeking always to reconcile different views (Mandela refused to engage in recrimination against his predecessors)
- ☐ **motivation**: through inspiring thoughts and images, giving everyone a personal interest in making change happen
- ☐ **ambition**: visions should set stretching, but achievable targets ('out of reach, but not out of sight')
- ☐ **commitment**: leaders have to lead by example and give personal commitment to change (Mandela had shown huge courage throughout his life, and refused to make any deal with the government while a prisoner).

Read more:

Long Walk to Freedom

by Nelson Mandela

Mind pictures

Images and stories can be very useful tools in communicating about change. The benefits include:

- they are **memorable** in a way that facts and figures often aren't
- they **appeal** to our innate liking for narrative and hearing stories
- they can **simplify** concepts that in reality are highly complex (technically, socially, politically or organisationally) in such a way that people see through complexity to the heart of what needs to change
- by referring to characters, situations or metaphors that people **recognise**, they reduce perceptions of change as unknown, uncertain and unsafe
- they act as 'hooks' for people's **interest**, appealing to their curiosity and encouraging them to find out more
- by setting up particular **emotional connotations**, they can help to push along helpful behaviours and attitudes, or root out negative ones.

Mind pictures:

Business idea	Mind picture
We are a large organisation and need to work hard to be responsive and agile	Our business is like an elephant, it needs to be more like a fox
People will buy this product to make a particular statement about their status	If this product was a car, it would be a Mercedes
We need to focus on long-term progress, not just quick wins	The story of the hare and the tortoise
We need to share negative information about our business to identify areas for change	We've spent too long with our heads in the sand
We need to change how we gain and retain customers	Paint a 'pen picture' of a day in the life of a customer, containing several general problems our company could solve for her

There are a number of ways to use the power of illustration in communications. The table opposite shows some relatively dry business ideas and the pictures that might be used to illustrate them. They could be worked up as the theme for presentations, seminars and other communications, or simply used in one-on-one meetings to add interest to what you say.

Looking back:

Key ideas from this chapter

- ☐ In planning change, always remember that communication is of key importance.
- ☐ Use communication to get people involved in change and overcome resistance.
- ☐ Carefully consider what people want to hear and how they want to hear it.
- ☐ Use the right medium for the message and the audience.
- ☐ Work with people's natural communication preferences.
- ☐ Use vision statements and images to give change a memorable unifying theme.

7 After the change

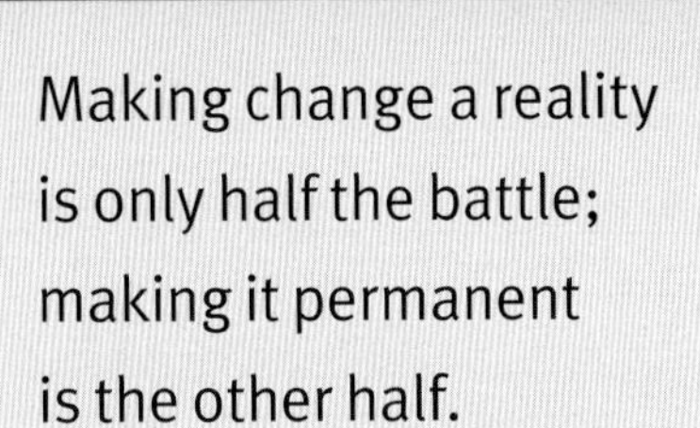

Making change a reality is only half the battle; making it permanent is the other half.

This chapter looks at ways that change can be 'made to stick'.

Quick wins

Quick wins are short-term, highly visible benefits of change. As well as being beneficial in themselves, they can also be helpful for change management, in a number of ways:

- they demonstrate that **change works**
- they show that **sacrifices are worthwhile**
- they show that **efforts are making a difference**
- they provide **reward and recognition** for those managing change and working towards its success
- they can **build momentum** by convincing those who resisted change and addressing people's concerns
- they bring a sense of **partial closure**: part of the change has been achieved, recorded and celebrated; it can't be undone.

It is always worth considering whether quick wins should be brought forward because of these benefits. It may be worth making some sacrifices in terms of practicality or timescales in order to achieve a quick win.

Quick wins should therefore be performance gains or concrete, objectively beneficial achievements that are bounded and discrete. Beginning a project or opening a discussion is not a quick win – such actions merely emphasise how far there is to go. Quick wins need to have a sense of completeness about them. There also needs to be a clear causal relationship between actions taken as part of the change effort and the quick win, so no one can say it might have happened anyway.

The benefits from quick wins need to be publicised as widely as possible. Ideally, they will be benefits that everyone feels some sense of ownership about, to generate a sense of collective achievement.

Recognition and reward

The way in which the business recognises and rewards individuals and teams needs to support the change and be in harmony with the changed state of the business, rather than reinforcing old ways of doing things.

Celebrating successful change is a good way to offer recognition without necessarily adding a material reward. It can be thought of as part of the communication effort. To offer more tangible rewards, performance management systems could set targets aligned with change aims, and offer rewards and incentives to those who achieve them. Rewarding individuals in new ways can reinforce new cultures or attitudes that support the change.

Recognition and reward are good ways to give something back to those who supported or worked for change. They send a strong signal that change is viewed as positive by management and that those who assist it are valued within the business.

Indicators of success

Once change is complete, or key milestones have been achieved, information needs to be sought on the success (or otherwise) of the change. Key aims should be revisited, and any indicators of success examined to see what the benefits of change have been. Some information will come from within the business, from performance and financial data and internal communications. Other indicators of success will come from external sources, such as customer satisfaction surveys.

Real life : Dell: keeping up the ante

Michael Dell started off in business by selling home-made computers from his university dormitory room. Twenty years on, PC manufacturer Dell has become a major player in the PC industry, with around $40 billion in sales and 40,000 employees. Michael Dell himself, just 39 years old at the time of writing, is worth over $17 billion.

Dell is not a particularly innovative company, nor one driven by a wonderfully inspiring vision. Its success is built on a direct-selling business model that undercuts competitors on price, backed up by a supply chain that, although geographically disparate, is incredibly tightly managed.

Dell the company seems to have taken much of its personality from that of its founder, focusing on results: growth, cost savings and profits from 'day one' of a product launch. A big part of this philosophy is the willingness to change – and to change again if things don't work out. New business avenues are aggressively sought out, but if they fail to deliver quickly, they are abandoned with the same ruthlessness.

Dell devotes a much smaller proportion of its revenue to new product development and future technologies than its competitors (1.3%, compared to 5.9% at IBM and 5.8% at Hewlett Packard). Dell's strength is reacting to, and capitalising on, market trends, rather than preparing for the 'next big thing'.

The key points of the Dell philosophy are:

- **results**: poor performance is not tolerated; only the best results will do
- **efficiency and economy**: saving money is a key objective, just as important as profits or growth
- **attitude**: everyone at Dell is expected to display the same focused, direct attitude as their founder, questioning and challenging everything and acknowledging mistakes
- **no big egos**: Dell people – like their leader – are expected to sacrifice their own interests and modify their character traits for the good of the business
- **no complacency**: success is appreciated, but seen as a stepping-stone to greater things; as Michael Dell says: 'Celebrate for a nanosecond. Then move on'
- **no face-saving**: if new ventures fail to deliver, the plug is pulled or they get redesigned – fast.

As we saw in chapter 5, this kind of results-focused mercenary culture has its drawbacks. While certain types of people work well in a 'boiler room' atmosphere, others find that constant pressure and scant appreciation offer too little motivation and too much stress.

So, while you may feel you lack the inclination – or the strength – to drive your business to become another Dell, there may be much to learn from the philosophy of keeping up the ante and looking for new change opportunities all the time.

Concrete indicators, such as turnover, profit and output volumes, will be crucial, but 'soft' indicators can also be very useful and their importance should not be neglected. A change in how the business is perceived – from within or without – could be crucial to its future success, as might its capability to innovate or attract talented people. All these are difficult to quantify, but crucial to success nonetheless.

Keeping up the ante

Successful change should always be celebrated. Whatever the demands of day-to-day work pressures, time should be taken to recognise the contribution of those who have made change happen, and the business benefits that have resulted. They will want to feel that any sacrifices they have made, or extra effort they have put in, has been worthwhile.

However, celebration should not be allowed to become complacency. As we saw in chapter 2, change is about constant evolution. The process of change is never 'over' in the sense of the business arriving at its ideal state.

More changes will be necessary; indeed, the need for further change may have been highlighted by the change process itself. But the danger is that repeated change results in change fatigue, cynicism and resistance. One of the most important benefits of good change management is to pave the way for future change, as well as achieving the objectives at hand. Change isn't just about embedding specific aims – it's about establishing new attitudes and beliefs about change itself.

The less pain involved in change, the more likely it is that people will endorse future changes. Change managers who set realistic boundaries and targets, hit key milestones and achieve their aims are more likely to be successful in generating commitment for future changes. 'Short sharp shock' changes, however effective in structural or technical terms, may be less likely to build commitment for future changes.

You should aim to make change a normal part of management and business life rather than an exceptional situation. As well as being committed to the specific changes undertaken, people need to become committed to the concept of change as a force for good – as something that brings business and individual benefits. This may not be easy or quick to achieve, but if it can be brought about the benefits to the business are immense. If everyone is actively looking for positive changes to make in their area of influence, and sees benefit in making them happen or suggesting them, the agility and responsiveness of the business can only improve.

A big part of this is maintaining the emphasis on listening and acting on people's opinions; they will certainly become cynical if it becomes clear to them that their opinions were only sought to 'oil the wheels' of change and are irrelevant thereafter. If people's opinions are important to change, and change needs to be constant, then it follows that the listening and co-operation should not stop once change aims have been achieved.

We hope that the learning and techniques contained in this book will help you to adapt and transform your business effectively, and make relatively pain-free change and growth an integral part of your organisation in the future.

Looking back:

Key ideas from this chapter

- ☐ Go for quick wins to show that change works and is bringing benefits to the business.
- ☐ Recognise and reward those who have made change happen.
- ☐ Look for signs that change is working.
- ☐ Keep up the ante by looking for new changes to make all the time and maintaining the emphasis on listening and co-operation that made change successful.

Index

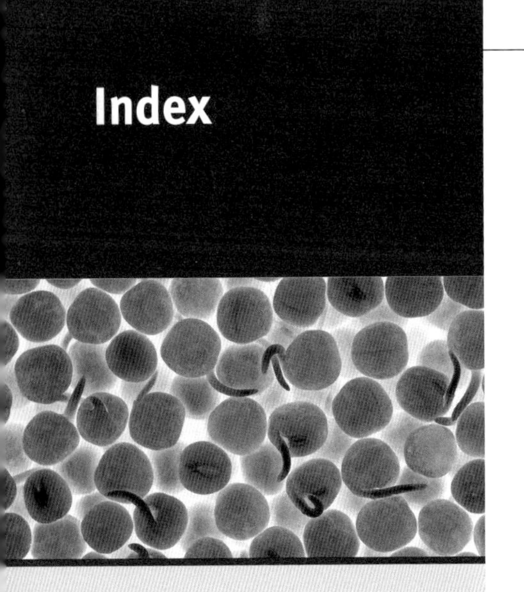